SPIRITUAL WARFARE

DEFEAT YOUR ENEMY AND LIVE A VICTORIOUS LIFE IN CHRIST

Apostle Antonio M. Palmer

SPIRITUAL WARFARE
Defeat Your Enemy and Live a Victorious Life in Christ

Published by
Kingdom Publishing, LLC
Odenton, Maryland U.S.A.

Printed in the U.S.A.

2023 revision of the Introduction to Spiritual Warfare workbook,
copyrighted ©2016 by Antonio M. Palmer
The Introduction to Spiritual Warfare course was first taught by Bishop Antonio Palmer in 2010.

All rights reserved.
No part of this book may be reproduced or transmitted in any form or by any means without written permission of the author.

Cover design by Kingdom Publishing, LLC

ISBN: 978-1-947741-88-1

TABLE OF CONTENT

Lesson 1: What is Spiritual Warfare?

Lesson 2: Our Three Enemies

- Enemy #1: Lucifer (Satan)
- Enemy #2: The World
- Enemy #3: The Flesh

Lesson 3: The Origin of Our Enemies

Lesson 4: How to Defeat the Enemy [Part 1: The Whole Armor of God]

- The Belt of Truth
- The Breastplate of Righteousness
- The Shoes of the Preparation of the Gospel of Peace
- The Shield of Faith
- The Sword of the Spirit
- The Helmet of Salvation

Lesson 5: How to Defeat the Enemy [Part 2: The Weapons of Our Warfare]

- Acknowledging the Fight
- Ten Spiritual Weapons
- Four Things to Use Your Weapons Against

Lesson 6: Overcomers and Their Rewards

- Eat from the Tree of Life
- The Crown of Life
- Eat of the Hidden Manna
- A White Stone with a New Name Written on It
- Authority Over the Nations
- Clothed in White Garments
- The Book of Life
- A Pillar in God's Temple
- Sharing in Christ's Throne

» Ephesians 6 Chart
» Different Types of Demonic Spirits
» Names, titles, Descriptions and Symbols of Satan in the Bible

- - - Spiritual Warfare—Defeat Your Enemy and Live a Victorious Life - - -

THE HELMET OF SALVATION

LESSON 1
WHAT IS SPIRITUAL WARFARE?

In your own words, what does the biblical term *Spiritual Warfare* mean to you?

_____
_____

Spiritual Warfare means:

_____
_____

1. **SPIRITUAL WARFARE** is _____. The fight against our spiritual enemies and his cohorts must be taken seriously. The enemy is _____ personally.

Scripture Relevance:

> "The thief cometh not but for to steal, and to kill, and to destroy: I am come that they may have life, and that they may have it more abundantly"
> (John 10:10).

The enemy has a personal vendetta against you. He wants to steal from You, kill You and destroy You!

Can you think of any reasons why the enemy is out to steal-kill-destroy you?

1. _____
2. _____
3. _____
4. _____
5. _____

Without coming to the realization that spiritual warfare is a personal fight, you may find yourself deceived and defeated, living life as a mere spectacle. Satan wants to leave you totally desolate and depleted of all the abundant life that is availabel to you through faith in Yeshua haMashiach (Jesus Christ).

2. **SPIRITUAL WARFARE INVOLVES AN _____ _____ AGAINST YOUR ENEMIES.**

Scripture Relevance

> "Submit yourselves therefore to God [Elohim].
> Resist the devil, and he will flee from you"
> James 4:7

Satan has initiated and unleashed an all-out attack against your life. You must fight back with a _____.

Because of your _____, your carnal mind craves things that are not spiritually healthy for you. In fact, those cravings are what make vulnerable to sin. Satan tempts us with the things that our flesh (fallen nature) finds most pleasurable. If we succumb to the temptation, we will find ourselves in sin.

3. TEMPTATION AND SIN

Temptation means:
_____
_____

Sin means:
_____
_____

The difference between being tempted and falling into sin:
_____
_____
_____
_____

Many believers do not differentiate between being tempted and sinning. I often hear, "I struggle with such-and-such sin." In actuality, the sin is not the struggle. Rather, it is the result of losing the fight with a particular temptation. Sin _____ against your spiritual enemy. Fortunately, when we confess our sins, Yeshua is faithful and just to forgive us of our sins and to cleanse us from ALL unrighteousness (1 John 1:9).

The opposite of sin is _____. Obedience is the result of winning the temptation battle. Obedience is the result of _____ against the enemy.

The key to spiritual warfare is being able to be victorious in temptation. Yeshua is our example of how to conquer temptation. Obedience to our heavenly father, Yahweh Elohim, is what the war is all about!

All temptation comes from Satan (and his cohorts that he assigns to you). He carries the title of the _____.

"Then was Jesus (Yeshua) led up of the Spirit into the wilderness to be tempted of the devil. And when he had fasted forty days and forty nights, he was afterward an hungered. And when the tempter came to him, he said..." (Matthew 4:1-3).

Every man is tempted when his attention is _____ with his fleshly desires.

"Blessed is the man that endureth temptation: for when he is tried, he shall received a crown of life, which the Lord hath promised to them that love him. Let no man say when he is tempted, I am tempted of God [Elohim]: for God [Elohim] cannot be tempted with evil, neither tempteth he any man. But every man is tempted, when he is drawn away of his own lust, and enticed. Then when lust hath conceived, it bringeth forth sin: and sin, when it is finished, bringeth forth death. Do not err, my beloved brethren" (James 1:12-16).

4. FROM TEMPTATION TO DEATH

Temptation is like a deceitful woman who is out for everything you got.

1. She will _____ you until you give in to her flattering demands.
2. Through your relations with her, you _____ a child called, "_____."
3. Sin is cute baby that grows up to become so disrespectful and dishonorable to you that you _____ from the sorrow and disappointment that it caused you.

5. NO UNCOMMON TEMPTATION

"There hath no temptation taken you but such as is common to man: but God [Elohim] is faithful, who will not suffer you to be tempted above that ye are able; but will with the temptation also make a way to escape, that ye may be able to bear it" (1 Corinthians 10:13).

There are five (5) things we can learn from this passage of Scripture:

1. There is no _____.
2. God [Elohim] is _____ and will not allow you to be tempted above what you are able to handle.
3. Every temptation has an _____ (a way out). Never say you're stuck, there's always a way out. You just have to find the exit door.
4. The phrase *"a way of escape"* is used to translate the Greek word *ekbasis*. In early Greek usage, this term had the sense of a landing place for a ship. The idea is not that Yah will enable us to escape temptation, but that he will enable us to land intact on the other side.
5. The purpose for the way of escape is to reassure our _____. If we know that we can have a safe place to land our ship it gives us confidence to stay the course. Knowing we have a way of escape in every temptation gives us confidence that what we are going through is _____ at the end. Thus, *"ye are able to bear it."*

THE BREASTPLATE OF RIGHTEOUSNESS

LESSON 2
OUR THREE ENEMIES

1. THE NATURE OF MAN

To gain a better understanding of why all who believe in Jesus Christ go through what is known as "spiritual warfare," we should study the first and original creation of man.

First, the Scriptures clearly and distinctly teach that man was _____ by _____ (Genesis 1:27; 2:7).

Scripture Reference

"So God created man in His own _____, in the image of God created He him; male and female created He them" (Genesis 1:27)

Genesis 2:7
"And the Lord God formed man of the dust of the ground, and breathed into his nostrils the breath of life; and man became a living soul" (Genesis 2:7).

1. The dust of the ground - _____
2. The breath *(Heb. neshamah)* of life *(Heb. chayay)* - _____
3. The living soul - _____

Note: Attention has been called to the occurrence of the Hebrew verb for create (bara) in Genesis 1:27, showing the absolute separation of mankind from the animal kingdom. The animals were _____. No animal was considered to be _____.

In order to understand spiritual warfare you must understand that you were made in the image of God. You will learn that the fight is about the image that God put in you that your enemy seeks to destroy, which was restored by Jesus Christ.

2. THE FIRST FIGHT

The Lord God prepared a garden eastward in Eden for Adam. He told him to dress and _____ it. The word *keep* is a very important word that God used while instructing Adam. The Hebrew word for *"keep"* is *"shamar"* which means to _____. Why do you think God told Adam to safeguard the garden?

_____

_____

_____

_____

The Lord further instructs Adam, *"Of every tree of the garden thou mayest freely eat: but of the tree of the knowledge of good and evil, thou shalt not eat of it: for in the day that thou eatest thereof thou shalt surely die"* (Genesis 2:16-17).

In Genesis 3, we get first glimpse of the intruder, the first enemy.

> "Now the serpent was more subtil than any beast of the field which the Lord God had made. And he said unto the woman. Yea, hath God said, Ye shall not eat of every tree of the garden? And the woman said unto the serpent, We may eat of the fruit of the trees of the garden: but of the fruit of the tree which is in the midst of the garden, God hath said, Ye shall not eat of it, neither shall ye touch it, lest ye die. And the serpent said unto the woman, Ye shall not surely die: for God doth know that in the day ye eat thereof, then your eyes shall be opened, and ye shall be as gods, knowing good and evil. And when the woman saw that the tree was good for food, and that it was pleasant to the eyes, and a tree to be desired to make one wise, she took of the fruit thereof, and did eat, and gave also unto her husband with her; and he did eat. And the eyes of them both were opened, and they knew that they were naked; and they sewed fig leaves together, and made themselves aprons" (Genesis 3:1-7).

The enemy's objective was to get man to _____ God. The _____ of God was forfeited by Adam when he disobeyed God's instruction. When the image of God was forfeited, Adam's _____ was stripped from him. He no longer dominion over the earth. The serpent stole the authority and Adam became subservient to the serpent.

3. TEMPTATION

The first fight came by way of a _____. There is no warfare without a temptation.

What is a temptation?

_____
_____
_____
_____

1 John 2:15, 16 reveal three elements of temptation.

> "Love not the world, neither the things that are in the world. If any man love the world, the love of the Father is not in him. For all that is in the world, the lust of the flesh, and the lust of the eyes, and the pride of life, is not of the Father, but is of the world."

1. The lust of the flesh - _____
2. The lust of the eyes - _____
3. The pride of life - _____

Thus, whenever we speak of spiritual warfare we essentially speak of the enemy's tactic against us that ultimately comes in the form of a temptation.

"Greater is he that is in you, than he that is in the world."
1 JOHN 4:4

4. God Officially Declares War on the Enemy

Genesis 3:14-15

> "And the Lord God said unto the serpent, Because thou hast done this, thou art cursed above all cattle, and above every beast of the field; upon thy belly shalt thou go, and dust shalt thou eat all the days of thy life: and I will put enmity between thee and the woman, and between thy seed and her seed; *it shall bruise thy head,* and thou shalt bruise his heel." (italics added for emphasis)

God said He will put _____ between the serpent and the woman. This enmity indicates that He was declaring war against the serpent for tempting man to disobey God. The results of the warfare will be:

1. _____
2. _____

The seed of the woman that would bruise the serpents head is _____. The serpent has been trying to destroy the seed of the woman every since the prophetic word was released from the mouth of God.

5. Enemy #1

Genesis 3 reveals that the intruder who was in Adam's garden came by way of the serpent. But who was he really? And how do you know?

_____
_____
_____
_____
_____

6. Enemy #2

The _____ or *kosmos* often refers to the vast system of this age which Satan promotes and which exists _____. It consists not only in the obviously evil, immoral, and sinful pleasures of the world, but also refers to a spirit of rebellion, resistance, or indifference to God and His revelation that exists within all human enterprises that are NOT under the Lordship of Jesus Christ. In this age Satan uses the world's ideas, morality, philosophies, psychology, desires, governments, media, religions, sports, culture, education, science, art, medicine, music, economic systems, entertainment, agriculture, etc. to oppose God, His people, His Word and His righteous standards. Satan has organized the world into political, cultural, economic, and religious systems that are _____ toward God and His people.

List some ways that Satan uses the "world" to promote evil and rebellion against God:

1. Government

2. Media

3. Music

4. Education

5. Religion

6. Economy

It is set up to be at odds against you and you must _____ it in order to produce any God-kind of results in your life.

Scriptures concerning Satan's hostile system:

_____: "In whom the god of this world hath blinded the minds of them which believe not, lest the light of the glorious gospel of Christ, who is the image of God, should shine unto them."

_____: "Wherein in time past ye walked according to the course of this world, according to the prince of the power of the air, the spirit that now worketh in the children of disobedience."

_____: "These things I have spoken unto you, that in me ye might have peace. In the world ye shall have tribulation: but be of good cheer; I have overcome the world."

_____: "And be not conformed to this world: but be ye transformed by the renewing of your mind, that ye may prove what is that good, and acceptable, and perfect, will of God."

_____: "Love not the world, neither the things that are in the world. If any man love the world, the love of the Father is not in him. For all that is in the world, the lust of the flesh, and the lust of the eyes, and the pride of life, is not of the Father, but is of the world."

_____: "Ye are of God, little children, and have overcome them: because greater is he that is in you, than he that is in the world."

_____: "For whatsoever is born of God overcometh the world: and this is the victory that overcometh the world, even our faith. Who is he that overcometh the world, but he that believeth that Jesus is the Son of God?"

"For I reckon that the sufferings of this present time are not worthy to be compared with the glory which shall be revealed in us."
ROMANS 8:18

7. Enemy #3

The third enemy that you face and must overcome is _____.
The flesh (Gk. *Sarx* or *Sarkos*) is the sinful element in human nature with its corrupt desires. It is the _____ nature of Man. It remains within the Christian after his conversion and is a deadly enemy to him. Satan, his emissaries and his worldly system are all _____ enemies, but the flesh is _____.

Romans 8:1-14

"There is therefore now no condemnation to them which are IN Christ Jesus, who walk not after _____, but after _____. For the law of the Spirit of life IN Christ Jesus hath made me free from the law of _____. For what the law could not do in that it was weak through the flesh, God sending His own Son in the likeness of sinful flesh, and for sin, condemned sin in the flesh: That the righteousness of the law might be fulfilled IN US, who walk not after the flesh, but after the Spirit. For they that are after the flesh _____; but they that are after the Spirit the things of the Spirit. For to be _____ is death; but to be spiritually minded is life and peace. Because the carnal mind is _____ against God; for it is not subject to the law of God, neither indeed can be. So then they that are in the flesh _____. But ye are not in the flesh, but in the Spirit, if so be that the Spirit of God dwell in you. Now if any man have not the Spirit of Christ, he is none of His. And if Christ be in you, the body is dead because of sin; but the Spirit is life because of righteousness. But if the Spirit of Him that raised up Jesus from the dead dwell in you, He that raised up Christ from the dead shall also quicken your mortal bodies by His Spirit that dwelleth in you. Therefore, brethren, we are debtors, not to the flesh, to live after the flesh. For if ye live after the flesh, ye shall ____: but if ye through the Spirit do mortify the deeds of the body, ye shall live. For as many as are led by the Spirit of God, they are the sons of God."

Galatians 5:13-21

"For, brethren, ye have been called unto liberty; only _____ _____, but by love serve one another. For all the law is fulfilled in one word, even in this; Thou shalt love thy neighbor as thyself. But if ye bite and devour one another, take heed that ye be not consumed one of another. This I say then, walk in the Spirit, and ye shall not fulfil _____ of the flesh. For the flesh _____ the Spirit, and the Spirit _____ the flesh: and these are _____ the one to the other: so that _____. But if ye be led of the Spirit, ye are not under the law. Now the works of the flesh are _____, which are these; adultery, fornication, uncleanness, lasciviousness, idolatry, witchcraft, hatred, variance, emulations, wrath, strife, seditions, heresies, envying, murders, drunkenness, revellings, and such like: of which I tell you before, as I have also told you in time past, that they which do such things _____ inherit the kingdom of God."

Galatians 6:7-8

"Be not _____; God is not _____: for whatsoever a man soweth, that shall he also reap. For he that soweth to his flesh shall of the flesh reap _____; but he that soweth to the Spirit shall of the Spirit reap life everlasting."

Ephesians 2:1-3

"And You hat he quickened, who were dead in trespasses and sins; wherein in time past ye walked according to _____, according to _____ _____, the spirit that now worketh in the children of _____: among whom also we all had our conversation in times past in the lusts of our flesh, fulfilling the desires of the flesh and of the mind; and were by nature the children of _____, even as others."

18 Things you should know about the flesh:

1. _____
2. _____
3. _____
4. _____
5. _____

6. _____
7. _____
8. _____
9. _____
10. _____
11. _____
12. _____
13. _____
14. _____
15. _____
16. _____
17. _____
18. _____

How can a believer *sow* to his flesh?

_____
_____
_____
_____

HOMEWORK

What are some of the battles that you have with YOUR FLESH that rages against the Spirit?

_____
_____
_____
_____
_____
_____

THE SANDALS OF THE PREPARATION OF THE GOSPEL OF PEACE

LESSON 3
THE ORIGIN OF OUR ENEMIES

When it comes to spiritual warfare, it is wise to gain knowledge of your enemy and his tactics. In Eternity, before time began and before God created the Earth, He created other living beings called _____. There are innumerable angels (Deuteronomy 33:2, Psalm 68:17, Daniel 7:10, Luke 2:13, Hebrews 12:22, Revelation 5:11). In the Bible, angels were sometimes called _____ (Genesis 6:2, Job 38:7) and _____ (Job 1:6; 2:1; 38:7, Isaiah 14:13, Revelation 12:4). Angels may be defined as an order of _____.
The word angel in Hebrew (Malachim) and in Greek (aggelos) both mean _____.

1. **The Nature of Angels**

    1. _____
    2. _____
    3. _____
    4. _____
    5. _____
    6. _____
    7. _____
    8. _____
    9. _____

In the Bible, there are three known archangels:

   ✶_____   ✶_____   ✶_____

1. The Origin of Satan

Ezekiel 28:11-19

"Moreover the word of the LORD came unto me, saying, Son of man, take up a lamentation upon *the king of Tyrus,* and say unto him, Thus saith the Lord GOD; Thou sealest up the sum, *full of wisdom,* and *perfect in beauty. Thou hast been in Eden the garden of God; every precious stone was thy covering,* the sardius, topaz, and the diamond, the beryl, the onyx, and the jasper, the sapphire, the emerald, and the carbuncle, and gold: the workmanship of *thy tabrets* and of *thy pipes* was prepared in thee in the day that thou wast created. Thou art *the anointed cherub that covereth;* and I have set thee so: thou wast upon the holy mountain of God; thou hast walked up and down in the midst of the stones of fire. *Thou wast perfect in thy ways* from the day that thou wast created, till *iniquity was found in thee.* By the multitude of thy merchandise they have filled the midst of thee with violence, and thou hast sinned: therefore I will cast thee as profane out of the mountain of God: and I will destroy thee, O covering cherub, from the midst of the stones of fire. *Thine heart was lifted up* because of thy beauty, thou hast *corrupted thy wisdom* by reason of thy brightness: I will cast thee to the ground, I will lay thee before kings, that they may behold thee. Thou hast defiled thy sanctuaries by the multitude of thine iniquities, by the iniquity of thy traffick; therefore will I bring forth a fire from the midst of thee, it shall devour thee, and I will bring thee to ashes upon the earth in the sight of all them that behold thee. All they that know thee among the people shall be astonished at thee: thou shalt be a terror, and never shalt thou be any more."

What did we learn about Satan here in Ezekiel 28? (According to the 66 books of the Kings James Version [KJV]. Other angels are listed in the Apocrypha)

1. _____
2. _____
3. _____
4. _____
5. _____
6. _____

7. _____
8. _____

2. Lucifer's Fall

Iniquity was found in Lucifer and he became filled with _____ and he sinned. His heart was lifted up because of his _____ and his wisdom was corrupted (twisted) by his own _____ (he started thinking of himself highly than he ought).

He was cast out of the mountain of God and God declared that He will destroy Lucifer from the midst of the stones of fire.

Luke 10:17, 18

"And the seventy returned again with joy, saying, Lord, even the devils are subject unto us through thy name. And he said unto them, _____
_____."

Isaiah 14:12-17

"How art thou fallen from heaven, O Lucifer, son of the morning! how art thou cut down to the ground, which didst weaken the nations! For thou hast said in thine heart, I will ascend into heaven, I will exalt my throne above the stars of God: I will sit also upon the mount of the congregation, in the sides of the north: I will ascend above the heights of the clouds; I will be like the most High. Yet thou shalt be brought down to hell, to the sides of the pit. They that see thee shall narrowly look upon thee, and consider thee, saying, Is this the man that made the earth to tremble, that did shake kingdoms; that made the world as a wilderness, and destroyed the cities thereof; that opened not the house of his prisoners?"

Lucifer speaks his heart: *"Out of the abundance of the heart, the mouth speaks."*

1. _____
2. _____

3. _____
4. _____
5. _____

Note: At the time of Lucifer's fall, he was then known as the Satan. Satan literally means adversary or accuser.

3. Angels Fall with Lucifer (Satan)

Revelation 12:1-11

"And there appeared a great wonder in heaven; a woman clothed with the sun, and the moon under her feet, and upon her head a crown of twelve stars: And she being with child cried, travailing in birth, and pained to be delivered. And there appeared another wonder in heaven; and behold *a great red dragon*, having seven heads and ten horns, and seven crowns upon his heads. And *his tail drew the third part of the stars of heaven, and did cast them to the earth:* and the dragon stood before the woman which was ready to be delivered, for to devour her child as soon as it was born. And she brought forth a man child, who was to rule all nations with a rod of iron: and her child was caught up unto God, and to his throne. And the woman fled into the wilderness, where she hath a place prepared of God, that they should feed her there a thousand two hundred and threescore days. And there was war in heaven: Michael and his angels fought against the dragon; and the dragon fought and his angels, And prevailed not; neither was their place found any more in heaven. And the great dragon was cast out, that old serpent, called the Devil, and Satan, which deceiveth the whole world: he was cast out into the earth, and his angels were cast out with him. And I heard a loud voice saying in heaven, Now is come salvation, and strength, and the kingdom of our God, and the power of his Christ: for the accuser of our brethren is cast down, which accused them before our God day and night. And they overcame him by the blood of the Lamb, and by the word of their testimony; and they loved not their lives unto the death."

"Behold, what manner of love the Father hath bestowed upon us, that we should be called the sons of God."
1 JOHN 3:1

Seven things revealed about Satan in Revelation 12:1-11

1. _____
2. _____
3. _____
4. _____
5. _____
6. _____
7. _____

Additional notes:
_____
_____
_____
_____

4. Fallen Angels, Giants and Demons

FALLEN ANGELS

Christians adopted the concept of fallen angels mainly based on their interpretations of the Book of Revelation Chapter 12.

The Catechism of the Catholic Church speaks of "the fall of the angels" not in spatial terms but as a radical and irrevocable rejection of God and his reign by some angels who, though created as good beings, freely chose evil, their sin being unforgivable because of the irrevocable character of their choice, not because of any defect in the infinite divine mercy.[1]

---

[1] The Catechism of the Catholic Church, "The Fall of Angels" (391-395), Vatican.va retrived 2012-07-03

Genesis 6:1-4 KJV

And it came to pass, when men began to multiply on the face of the earth, and daughters were born unto them, that the _____ saw the daughters of men that they were fair; and they took them wives of all which they chose. And the LORD said, My spirit shall not always strive with man, for that he also is flesh: yet his days shall be an hundred and twenty years. There were _____ in the earth in those days; and also after that, when the _____ came in unto the daughters of men, and they bare children to them, the same became mighty men which were of old, men of renown.

Genesis 6:1-4 THE MESSAGE BIBLE

When the human race began to increase, with more and more daughters being born, the sons of God noticed that the daughters of men were beautiful. They looked them over and picked out wives for themselves. Then God said, "I'm not going to breathe life into men and women endlessly. Eventually they're going to die; from now on they can expect a life span of 120 years." This was back in the days (and also later) when there were giants in the land. The giants came from the union of the sons of God and the daughters of men. These were the mighty men of ancient lore, the famous ones.

Daniel also refers to these fallen angels as "_____."

"This sentence is by the decree of *the angelic watchers* and the decision is a command of *the holy ones,* In order that the living may know that the Most High is ruler over the realm of mankind, And bestows it on whom He wishes And sets over it the lowliest of men."
(Daniel 4:7)

Who do you think are "the holy ones" that Daniel is refering to in this passage?

_____

It has been the opinion of rabbinical scholars, and the translators of the Septuagint *(a Greek translation of the Hebrew Bible made in the 3rd and 2nd centuries BC to meet the needs of Greek-speaking Jews (Judah) outside of Palestine)* that angels co-habited with the daughters of

Adam. The early church agreed with this view. Justin Martyr, Cyprian, Eusebius, and even _____ (a historical writer) accepted this view.

Justin Martyr (the earliest of the church fathers) in his Second Apology wrote, *"The angels lusted after woman, and beget giants. These giants upon death became the demons."*[2]

The cohabitation with human females resulted in an offspring called, "_____." King James calls them "Giants." Giants in Hebrew text are described as "_____ _____."

The fact that these fallen angels, who are *beings from another world,* could take upon themselves flesh is clearly evidenced by Abraham's conversation with the angels on their way to destroy Sodom and Gomorrah who appeared as humans and even ate natural, earthly food (Genesis 18).

Angels can change into physical form even though by nature they are spirit beings. The Bible does not tell us how this happens, but it refers to angels _____ _____ and "he hath reserved (them) in everlasting chains under darkness unto the judgment of the great day…even so Sodom and Gomorrah and cities about them in like manner, giving themselves over to fornication, and going after _____ _____" (Jude 6-7). Jude calls these angels who didn't keep their first estate as _____. Now we can see why there was tremendous violence on the earth in the days of Noah (Genesis 6:5-6).

Some will refute this doctrine of angels sleeping with women by citing Jesus when answering the Sadducees (those religious leaders who didn't believe in resurrection),

> "For when they shall rise from the dead, they neither marry, nor are given in marriage; but are as the angels which are in heaven." (Mark 12:25, Matthew 22:30)

---

[2] www.fallenangels-ckquarterman.com

But let's look at what Luke 20:34-36 says:

> "The sons of this age marry and are given in marriage, but those who are considered worthy to attain to that age and the resurrection from the dead, neither marry, nor are given in marriage; _____, for they are like angels, and are sons of God, being sons of the resurrection."

The reason why angels don't marry in heaven is because _____. There is no need for marriage in heaven because there is no need to _____. When men die or attain resurrection they are like the angels, not in the sense of physicality but in terms of _____. Jesus did not say that angels are _____ _____, but simply that they do not marry because they do not die. Sexual intercourse was commanded by God for the purpose of _____ ("be fruitful and multiply") or _____ through the institute of marriage. Satan and the fallen angels wanted to populate the Earth with _____ and not God's. Thus, on Earth, it still remains possible for men and angels to marry and have sex for procreation.

Hebrews 13:2 tells us that people have _____ _____! This means that angels can take on human appearance to such a convincing state that they can't be distinguished from people.

These angels were bound to _____.

2 Peter 2:4-5

> "For if God spared not the angels that sinned, but cast them down to _____ (Tartarus), and delivered them into chains of darkness, to be reserved unto judgment; and spared not the old world, but saved Noah the eighth person, a preacher of righteousness, bringing in the flood upon the world of the ungodly…"

"Who is this King of glory? YAHWEH strong and mighty, YAHWEH mighty in battle. Lift up your heads, O ye gates; even lift them up, ye everlasting doors; And the King of glory shall come in. Who is this King of glory? YAHWEH TZVA'OT, he is the King of glory." PSALM 24:8-10

5. THE ORIGIN OF THE GIANTS

Genesis 6:4 THE MESSAGE BIBLE

"This was back in the days (and also later) when there were *giants* in the land. The *giants* came from the union of the sons of God and the daughters of men. These were the mighty men of ancient lore, the famous ones."

Some time before the flood, between Adam's time and especially in Noah's days, the fallen angels did not keep their first estate and chose to manipulate the system and sleep with the daughters of men. The fallen angels' sexual relations with the daughters of men (women) produced a *hybrid race of people* called _____.

God destroyed the Giants from the face of the Earth along with wicked men. However, there was another set of angels that did not keep their first estate, and they again produced more giants after the Flood.

Genesis 6:4 says, "This was back in the days _____ when there were giants in the land.

GIANTS AFTER THE FLOOD

During the time of _____, the giants were called _____, _____, and _____. Abraham had to face giants!

Genesis 14:5

"And in the fourteenth year came Chedorlaomer, and the kings that were with him, and smote the *Rephaim* in Ashteroth Karnaim, and the *Zuzims* in Ham, and the *Emims* in Shaveh Kiriathaim."

Lot's daughters had sons born to him. The two sons were Moab and Ben Ammi. They produced nations called the _____ and the _____. During _____ days, giants were definitely in the land of Canaan.

"And there we saw the giants (Nephilim), the sons of Anak, which come of the giants (Nephilim): and we were in our own sight as grasshoppers, and so we were in their sight" (Numbers 13:33).

In Deuteronomy 2:11, also during the times of Moses and Joshua, the Moabites called the giants "Emims."

"Which also were accounted giants (Nephilim), as the Anakims; but the Moabites call them *Emims*" (Deuteronomy 2:11).

In Deuteronomy 2:20, the Ammonites called the giants "_____" (Gen. 14:5).

"(That also was accounted a land of giants: giants dwelt therein in old time; and the Ammonites call them *Zamzummims*;"(Deuteronomy 2:20).

"For only Og king of Bashan remained of the remnant of giants; behold, his bedstead was a bedstead of iron; is it not in Rabbath of the children of Ammon? _____ was the length thereof, and _____ the breadth of it, after the cubit of a man." (Deuteronomy 3:11)

"And the rest of Gilead, and all Bashan, being the kingdom of Og, gave I unto the half tribe of Manasseh; all the region of Argob, with all Bashan, which was called *the land of giants*" (Deuteronomy 3:13).

"All the kingdom of Og in Bashan, which reigned in Ashtaroth and in Edrei, who remained of the remnant of the giants: for these did _____, and cast them out" (Joshua 13:12).

"And the border went up by the valley of the son of Hinnom unto the south side of the Jebusite; the same is _____: and the border went up to the top of the mountain that lieth before the valley of Hinnom westward, which is at the end of the valley of the giants northward" (Joshua 15:8).

"And Joshua answered them, If thou be a great people, then get thee up to the wood country, and cut down for thyself there in the land of the Perizzites and of the giants, if mount Ephraim be too narrow for thee" (Joshua 17:15).

Remember when Noah got drunk after the flood and Ham saw his nakedness and God proclaimed a curse? What was the curse?

Genesis 9:25-27

Then He said, "_____
_____. And he said: Blessed be the Lord, the God of Shem, and may Canaan be his servant. May God enlarge Japheth, and may he dwell in the tents of Shem and may Canaan be his servant."

God only cursed _____ offspring, not Ham! Could it be that God foresaw the next set of angels leaving their natural state and sleeping with women all throughout the land of Canaan?

Then in Genesis 15:13-21, God says this to Abraham,

"And he said unto Abram, Know of a surety that thy seed shall be a stranger in a land that is not theirs, and shall serve them; and they shall afflict them four hundred years; And also that nation, whom they shall serve, will I judge: and afterward shall they come out with great substance. And thou shalt go to thy fathers in peace; thou shalt be buried in a good old age. But in the fourth generation they shall come hither again: _____
_____. And it came to pass, that, when the sun went down, and it was dark, behold a smoking furnace, and a burning lamp that passed between those pieces. In the same day the LORD made a covenant with Abram, saying, Unto thy seed have I given this land, from the river of Egypt unto the great river, the river Euphrates: The Kenites, and the Kenizzites, and the Kadmonites, And the Hittites, and the Perizzites, and the Rephaims, And the Amorites, and the Canaanites, and the Girgashites, and the Jebusites."

By the time that Abraham's descendants reached the land of Canaan it was immersed with the hybrid half angel-half man race of people called *Nephilim* from as far south as Jericho to as far north as Gath of the Philisitines. The fulfillment of both Canaan's curse and Abraham's blessing!

God told Joshua to _____! Why?
_____
_____

There were giants living during the time of David.

> "Then a champion came out from the armies of the Philistines named _____, from Gath, whose height was _____" (1 Samuel 17:4).

> "Moreover the Philistines had yet war again with Israel; and David went down, and his servants with him, and fought against the Philistines: and David waxed faint. And Ishbibenob, which was of the sons of the giant, the weight of whose spear weighed three hundred shekels of brass in weight, he being girded with a new sword, thought to have slain David. But Abishai the son of Zeruiah succoured him, and smote the Philistine, and killed him. Then the men of David sware unto him, saying, Thou shalt go no more out with us to battle, that thou quench not the light of Israel. And it came to pass after this, that there was again a battle with the Philistines at Gob: then Sibbechai the Hushathite slew Saph, which was of the sons of the giant. And there was again a battle in Gob with the Philistines, where Elhanan the son of Jaareoregim, a Bethlehemite, slew the brother of Goliath the Gittite, the staff of whose spear was like a weaver's beam. And there was yet a battle in Gath, where was a man of great stature, that had on every hand _____, four and twenty in number; and he also was born to the giant. And when he defied Israel, Jonathan the son of Shimea the brother of David slew him. These four were born to the giant in Gath, and fell by the hand of David, and by the hand of his servants" (2 Samuel 21:15-22).

God told David the same thing that he told Joshua, "_____." King Saul's sin was that he didn't follow God's command to utterly destroy all those who were living in the land. Also, David conquered the one city that Joshua did not conquer. Do you know which city it was? _____

The sole purpose of Satan and his angelic cohorts to intermix with Mankind was _____
_____.

> "And I will put enmity between thee and the woman, and between thy seed and her seed; it shall bruise thy head, and thou shalt bruise his heel" (Genesis 3:15).

6. THE ORIGIN OF DEMONS

"They shall no longer sacrifice their sacrifices to the _____ with which they play the harlot. This shall be a permanent statute to them throughout their generations." (Leviticus 17:7)

"They sacrificed to _____ who were not God, To gods whom they have not known, _____ who came lately, _____." (Deuteronomy 32:17)

"They even sacrificed their sons and their daughters to the _____" (Psalms 106:37).

Demons in the Hebrew Bible are of two classes: the _____ ("hairy beings") and the _____. The *se'irim*, to which some Israelites offered sacrifices in the open fields, were satyr-like creatures, described as dancing in the wilderness (Isaiah 13:21, 34:14).

But wild beasts of the desert shall lie there; and their houses shall be full of doleful creatures; and owls shall dwell there, and _____ shall dance there. - (Isaiah 13:21)

The wild beasts of the desert shall also meet with the wild beasts of the island, and the _____ shall cry to his fellow; the screech owl also shall rest there, and find for herself a place of rest. - (Isaiah 34:14)

Sayir or Sa'ir – _____. He is known to the Greeks as the god, *Pan*. Pan means *"to pasture,"* and he is god of the fields, groves and woodlands. The Romans called him *Faunus* meaning *"the wild god."* And they said he could reveal the future. The Celtics called him *Dusios*.

Dusios was a god of fertility, sexuality, and love, worshiped in forest groves. Today, in Wicca, or modern witchcraft, he is *the horn-god*. He's now known as god of the witches.

The Israelites also _____ to the shedim (Deut. 32:17; Ps. 106:37).

The Hebrew word used in these verses is *"Shed"* from *Shud* which means _____
_____. Jesus said, "the enemy cometh not but to kill, and to steal, and to destroy" (John 10:10a).

According to the Jewish Encyclopedia, "In Chaldean mythology the seven evil deities were known as *shedu*, _____, represented in _____ form." They were represented as *winged bulls,* derived from the colossal bulls used as protective _____ (genies) of royal palaces. From Chaldea, the term *shedu* traveled to the Israelites. The writers of the Tanach (Old Testament) applied the word as dialogism to Canaanite deities.

In ancient Arabia, Pre-Islamic mythology did not differentiate between gods and demons. Jinns were considered _____ and had many human abilities, such as eating, drinking, and procreating.

In the New Testament the Greek word, _____ is often translated as devils or demons. They are also designated as _____. KJV has one verse translated as "gods" and the NASB uses the word, "deities." *Daimon* (demons) is found 63 times in the New Testament.

E.W. Vines writes concerning the Greek word *daimon*, which is translated demon in the New Testament as being derived _____ [Vines, Expository Dictionary of New Testament Words].³⁴

The pagan people of Lystra thought Paul and Barnabas were demons (gods or deities)!

---

3   Vines, Expository Dictionary of New Testament Words
4   http://tbm.org/origindemons.htm

"And they called Barnabas, *Jupiter;* and Paul, *Mercurius,* because he was the chief speaker" (Acts 14:12). (Jupiter was the Roman god identical to the Greek god, *Zeus* and Mercurius was Roman for the Greek god, *Hermes*)

Demons are the _____ evil spirits of the Nephilim (giants). They are *disembodied,* meaning _____.

Justin Martyr (an early Christian father from 100-160 AD) says that the origin of demons is "_____
_____."

Job 26:5

"The _____ (Heb. Rapha'im. Ghosts of the dead, shades, spirits) tremble under the waters and their inhabitants." [NASB]

"The _____ (dead ones) are formed, Beneath the waters, also their inhabitants."

"Behold _____ groan under the waters, and they that dwell with them." [Duoay-Rheims Bible]

"The _____ tremble beneath the water, with its creatures." [The Complete Jewish Bible]

After the flood of Noah demons were around, and seem to have been involved with people in many ways. One way they seem to have been involved with people was in _____.

1 Corinthians 10:19-21

"What am I saying then? That an idol is anything, or what is offered to idols is anything? Rather, that the things which the Gentiles sacrifice they sacrifice to _____ and not to God, and I do not want you to have fellowship with demons. You cannot drink the cup of the Lord and the cup of demons; you cannot partake of the Lord's Table and of the table of demons."

Even as early as the time of Jacob in Genesis (1900s BC) it is recorded that Laban had _____ (Gen 31:30). It seems that these idols were inspired by demons, and the worship of them must have involved _____ with demons. Many nations had idols and practiced idolatry, and demons seem to have been involved in all this, across the worldwide scope of many cultures.

In the time of Moses (1400s BC) God forbade the making of idols in the Ten Commandments:

Exodus 20:4-6

"Thou shalt not make unto thee any _____, or any likeness [of any thing] that [is] in heaven above, or that [is] in the earth beneath, or that [is] in the water under the earth: Thou shalt not bow down thyself to them, nor serve them: for I the LORD thy God [am] a jealous God, visiting the iniquity of the fathers upon the children unto the third and fourth [generation] of them that hate me; And shewing mercy unto thousands of them that love me, and keep my commandments."

God also forbade the Israelites to be involved with various types of magic, familiar spirits, and necromancy.

Leviticus 20:27

"A man also or woman that hath a familiar spirit, or that is a wizard, shall surely be put to death: they shall stone them with stones: their blood [shall be] upon them."

According to the Strong's Concordance, the word here for "familiar spirit" means _____ _____. If one considers that demons are actually the spirits of the dead giants (Nephilim), then it makes a lot of sense that it is demons who are being referenced to here as the "ghost, spirit of a dead one." And it is forbidden for God's people to "evoke the spirit of a dead one," or to have anything to do with a demon, let alone to become familiar, gain familiarity, with one. The term here for "wizard" is "one who has a familiar spirit" and "necromancer," is _____ _____.

Deuteronomy 18:9-12

"When thou art come into the land which the LORD thy God giveth thee, thou shalt not learn to do after the abominations of those nations. There shall not be found among you [any one] that maketh his son or his daughter to pass through the fire, [or] that useth divination, [or] an observer of times, or an enchanter, or a witch, Or a charmer, or a consulter with familiar spirits, or a wizard, or a necromancer. For all that do these things [are] an abomination unto the LORD: and because of these abominations the LORD thy God doth drive them out from before thee."

Some of these same terms are used again in Deuteronomy 18, forbidding the people to practice or to consult with anyone who practiced, having a relationship with a demon. God calls this an _____, and makes clear that those nations around at the time all did practice these things. As such we can know historically that demons were interacting with people all throughout the world in this time period, as familiar spirits in various magical practices.

In the time of Jesus many in Israel and the surrounding nations, had come to be demonized and a major part of Jesus' ministry was in casting demons out of those who were demonized, and thereby healing them.

Luke 11:14-20

"Jesus was driving out a demon that was mute. When the demon left, the man who had been mute spoke, and the crowd was amazed. But some of them said, "By Beelzebub, the _____, he is driving out demons." Others tested him by asking for a sign from heaven. Jesus knew their thoughts and said to them: "Any kingdom divided against itself will be ruined, and a house divided against itself will fall. If Satan is divided against himself, how can his kingdom stand? I say this because you claim that I drive out demons by Beelzebub. Now if I drive out demons by Beelzebub, by whom do your followers drive them out? So then, they will be your judges. But if I drive out demons by the finger of God, then the kingdom of God has come to you."

It stands to reason that demons had also been inflicting people in times prior to then, as there already were Jewish people who were driving out demons at the time, prior to Jesus doing so. Jesus also makes clear that _____ had power over the demons, and Jesus equates the "prince of demons" or "Beelzebub" to either be Satan, or be working for Satan. And so it becomes clear that the demons were working for Satan.

Further confirmation that demons were the disembodied spirits of the dead giants (Nephilim) is seen in that they seemed to be familiar with God having sent someone to _____ in punishment, in specific their angel fathers.

Luke 8:28-31

> "When he saw Jesus, he cried out and fell at his feet, shouting at the top of his voice, "What do you want with me, Jesus, Son of the Most High God? I beg you, don't torture me!" (For Jesus had commanded the evil spirit to come out of the man. For oftentimes it had caught him: and he was kept bound with chains and in fetters; and he brake the bands, and was driven of the devil into the wilderness.) Jesus asked him, "What is your name?" "_____," he replied, because _____ had gone into him. And they begged him repeatedly not to order them to go into _____."

The term here for Abyss is the same word that is used in Revelation, the same place where _____ are released from. And as we have covered, this is synonymous with the lowest part of the Earth mentioned in Ezekiel 31, and _____, the prison of the angels who sinned before the Flood. Thus, the demons are aware that their angel fathers or paternal ancestors are imprisoned in the Abyss, and fear being imprisoned there themselves.

It is also interesting to note that the demons _____. In many places the attitude of the demons towards Jesus seems to be one of _____, and they beg and entreat him to not torment them, asking if he is going to _____ them.

> "Ah! What do you want with us, Jesus of Nazareth? Have you come to destroy us? I know who you are–the Holy One of God!" (Luke 4:34)

> "And cried with a loud voice, and said, What have I to do with thee, Jesus, [thou] Son of the most high God? I entreat thee by God, that thou torment me not." (Mark 5:7)

That they seemed to be seriously afraid is confirmed in:

"You believe that there is one God. You do well. Even the demons believer and _____." (James 2:19)

As part of his ministry, Jesus gave authority to His disciples to cast out demons.

Matthew 10:1

"And when he had called unto [him] his twelve disciples, he gave them power [against] _____, to cast them out, and to heal all manner of sickness and all manner of disease."

Mark 6:12-13

And they went out, and preached that men should repent. And they cast out _____, and anointed with oil many that were sick, and healed [them].

Luke 10:17-20

"And the seventy returned again with joy, saying, Lord, even the _____ _____. And he said unto them, I beheld Satan as lightning fall from heaven. Behold, I give unto you power to tread on serpents and scorpions, and over all the power of the enemy: and nothing shall by any means hurt you. Notwithstanding in this rejoice not, that the spirits are subject unto you; but rather rejoice, because your names are written in heaven."

Jesus made clear that in the future His followers also would continue to cast out demons.

Mark 16:17

"And these signs shall follow them that believe; In my name shall they cast out devils; they shall speak with new tongues"

And believers did just that, such as Paul who is recorded to have cast out a demon in Jesus' name in Acts.

Acts 16:16-18

"Now it happened, as we went to prayer, that a certain slave girl _____ _____ met us, who brought her masters much profit by fortune-telling. This girl followed Paul and us, and cried out, saying, "These men are the servants of the Most High God, who proclaim to us the way of salvation." And this she did for many days. But Paul, greatly annoyed, turned and _____, "I command you in the name of Jesus Christ to come out of her." And he came out that very hour."

Difference Between Fallen Angels and Demons

Fallen angels have their own celestial bodies, therefore they have no need to inhabit bodies. Yet demons seek bodies desperately; and, if need be, they will settle for the bodies of animals (Mark 5:12-13).

Third, fallen angels have the ability to fly, but demons can only walk. Jesus says concerning demons, "When the unclean spirit is gone out of a man, he _____ _____ _____" (Matthew 12:43, KJV).

Demons walk, fallen angels fly.

7. SOME ATTRIBUTES OF DEMONS:

a. _____. This has led to some very conservative Christians considering religions from Asatru to Zoroastrianism as forms of Satan worship.

b. _____. Jesus is described as expelling demons many times during his ministry (e.g. Matthew 15:22 and 15:28; Luke 4:33-35; listed below). Jesus empowered his disciples to also expel demons (Matthew 10:1; listed below).

c. They are also capable of _____:
Mark 5:7-13: "Now there was there nigh unto the mountains a great herd of swine feeding. And all the devils besought him, saying, Send us into the swine, that we may enter into them. And forthwith Jesus gave them leave. And the unclean spirits went out, and entered into the swine: and the herd ran violently down a steep place into the sea, (they were about two thousand;) and were choked in the sea."

d. _____.
James 2:19: "Thou believest that there is one God; thou doest well: the devils also believe, and tremble."

e. Recognized that Jesus is the _____.
Luke 4:41: "and devils also came out of many, crying out, and saying, Thou art Christ the Son of God. And he rebuking them suffered them not to speak: for they knew that he was Christ."
Mark 1:24: "...what have we to do with thee, thou Jesus of Nazareth? art thou come to destroy us? I know thee who thou art, the Holy One of God."

f. Will influence some Christians to _____:
1 Timothy 4:1: "...in the latter times some shall depart from the faith, giving heed to seducing spirits, and doctrines of devils"

g. Are in a state of war with Christian believers:
Ephesians 6:12: "For we wrestle not against flesh and blood, but against principalities, against powers, against the rulers of the darkness of this world, against spiritual wickedness in high places."

h. Will persuade people to _____:
Acts 5:3: "But Peter said, Ananias, why hath Satan filled thine heart to lie to the Holy Ghost..."

8. THINGS THAT CAN CAUSE DEMON POSSESSION:

1. _____
2. _____
3. _____
4. _____

5. _____
6. _____
7. _____
8. _____
9. _____
10. _____
11. _____
12. _____
13. _____
14. _____
15. _____
16. _____
17. _____
18. _____
19. _____
20. _____
21. _____
22. _____
23. _____
24. _____
25. _____
26. _____
27. _____
28. _____

9. CASTING OUT DEMONS IS PART OF THE WORK OF THE KINGDOM:

"If I by Beelzebul cast out demons, by whom do your sons cast them out? For this reason they will be your judges. 'But if I cast out demons by the Spirit of God, _____" (Matthew 12:27-28).

• • • Spiritual Warfare—Defeat Your Enemy and Live a Victorious Life • • •

"And these signs shall follow them that believe; in My name shall _____; they shall speak with new tongues; they shall take up serpents; and if they drink any deadly thing, it shall not hurt them; they shall lay hands on the sick, and they shall recover" (Mark 16:17-18).

"Heal the sick, raise the dead, cleanse the lepers, _____. Freely you received, freely give" (Matthew 10:8).

> "BEHOLD I GIVE YOU POWER TO TREAD ON SERPENTS AND SCORPIONS, AND OVER ALL THE POWER OF THE ENEMY: AND NOTHING SHALL BY ANY MEANS HURT YOU" — LUKE 10:19

Spiritual Warfare—Defeat Your Enemy and Live a Victorious Life

THE GIRDLE (BELT) OF TRUTH

LESSON 4
HOW TO DEFEAT THE ENEMY (PART I): THE WHOLE ARMOR OF GOD

EPHESIANS 6:10-18

"Finally, my brethren, be strong in the Lord, and in the power of his might. Put on the whole armour of God, that ye may be able to stand against the wiles of the devil. For we wrestle not against flesh and blood, but against principalities, against powers, against the rulers of the darkness of this world, against spiritual wickedness in high places. Wherefore take unto you the whole armour of God, that ye may be able to withstand in the evil day, and having done all, to stand. Stand therefore, having your loins girt about with truth, and having on the breastplate of righteousness; and your feet shod with the preparation of the gospel of peace; above all, taking the shield of faith, wherewith ye shall be able to quench all the fiery darts of the wicked. And take the helmet of salvation, and the sword of the Spirit, which is the word of God: praying always with all prayer and supplication in the Spirit, and watching thereunto with all perseverance and supplication for all saints."

To do spiritual warfare you must receive and follow the commandment to be:

1. _____
2. _____

<u>Strong</u>: The New Testament word for "Strong (strength(en))" is the Greek word *Endunamoo*
To be strong means _____
_____
_____

Rev10/2023   45

Ephesians 3:16 says,
"That He would grant you, according to the riches of His glory, to be _____ with might by His Spirit in the inner man."

To have the inner man *strengthened* (or made strong) by the Spirit is to have our feelings, thoughts, and purposes placed more and more under His _____ so that the Spirit can _____ through us in greater measure. The purpose of this strengthening by the Spirit is fourfold:

1. _____
   _____
2. _____
   _____
3. _____
   _____
4. _____
   _____

<u>Might</u>: The New Testament word for "might" is the Greek word *ischus* which means "ability" derived from the Greek word *eschon* meaning "force" and the root *echo* meaning "to have, hold, or possess." So, when the bible speaks of might, it is refering to ability, force and what you possess.

   a. Force means *strength or energy exerted against a person or thing that* _____.
   b. Ephesians 1:19 ("working" (Gk. *Energeia*)): This word is only used in the NT when referring to _____ power, whether of God or of the devil.
   c. Psalms 24:7-11 says, "Lift up your heads, O ye gates; and be ye lift up, ye everlasting doors; and the King of _____ shall come in. Who is this King of glory? The Lord _____ and _____, the Lord mighty in battle. Lift up your heads, O ye gates; even lift them up, ye everlasting doors; and the King of glory shall come in. Who is this King of glory? The Lord of hosts, he is the King of glory. Selah."
      i. You should never go into battle without any _____
      ii. Might is always used for _____. "Strength and Might" helps you to obtain _____. There's no glory without victory.

■ ■ ■ Spiritual Warfare—Defeat Your Enemy and Live a Victorious Life ■ ■ ■

1. Ephesians 6:11 and Ephesians 6:13 both instruct us to "put on or take unto you" the _____ armor of God for two reasons:
   a. _____
      i. _____ (Gk. Methodeia) – methods, trickery, cunning arts, schemes, deceitful strategies. Methodeia is taken from two Greek words, Meta (meaning "with") and Hodeuo (meaning "to travel or a journey; method"). Hodeuo is derived from the root word Hodos which metaphorically means _____ _____ Wiles are deceitful schemes to take you off the course or way that God has for you pertaining to your conduct, thinking, feeling and deciding. Stay on track!
      ii. Of the _____ – Gk. Diabolos. _____. To slander someone means _____ _____

   b. _____
      i. To withstand means _____
      ii. What does it mean to actively oppose someone?
          To actively oppose means _____ _____
      iii. _____ – Gk. *hemera ho poneros*. It is a time full of peril or danger to the faith and steadfastness causing pain and trouble. It's wicked, malign, unethical, and of an evil nature.
           a. Paul says in Ephesians 5:16, "_____ the time, because the days are evil."
           b. How do we *"redeem the time"*? We _____, not as fools, but as wise (Eph. 5:15). Circumspectly (Gk. blepo) means carefully, with discernment, with a watchful eye. Fools (the unwise) don't pay attention. We have to pay attention and keep a watchful eye on the enemy and his tactics in order to *withstand* him.

   Without the _____ of God (Gk. *Panoplian*) we will not be able to stand firm, hold our ground against every systematic, deceitful method and strategy coming against our character or reputation; neither actively oppose nor resist the devil at the time he tempts us or tries us. The Panoplian (full armor) of God is needed for the *methodeia* (deceitful strategies) of the devil.

c. For we wrestle (struggle) not against flesh and blood, but against principalities, against powers, against the rulers of the darkness of this world, against spiritual wickedness in heavenly places. _____
_____

d. The enemy must be met with _____. He must be forcefully _____. This is what is meant by James 4:7, "_____ yourselves therefore to God. _____ the devil, and he will _____ from you." In order to resist the devil you must _____.

e. The word "submit" is the Greek *"hypotasso"* which was a Greek military term meaning, _____
_____. The enemy doesn't run from us because we are sometimes _____. Submitting to God means to arrange your life back into the order that Christ, our Commander-in-chief instructed you to have it. It carries a non-military meaning of _____
_____
_____

» _____
_____
» _____
_____
» _____
_____
» _____
_____

If you want to know how to actively oppose the enemy or get involved in the fight just look at:

» _____
_____
» _____
_____
» _____
_____

THE WHOLE ARMOUR OF GOD

Without the whole (complete) armour of God it will be impossible for us to live a victorious life in Christ. The whole armour of God consists of six pieces which are:

1. _____
2. _____
3. _____
4. _____
5. _____
6. _____

1. **ARMOR PIECE #1: THE BELT OF TRUTH**

In the ancient garment of Paul's day, the belt (girdle) about the loins held in place every other part of the soldier's uniform. If the girdle was lost, you lost everything. In the armor of God, this girdle or belt is called _____. Truth holds everything together. This word "truth" is the Greek *aletheia* which alludes to reality and certainty but subjectively means _____ _____

   a. "Behold, thou (God) desirest _____ in the _____; and in the hidden parts thou will make me know wisdom" (Psalms 51:6). The Hebrew word for truth here is 'emeth which means _____ _____ _____ _____ It alludes to a character of _____.
   b. Read and Discuss Job 2:3, 9
   c. Read and Discuss Psalm 15:1, 2
   d. "Let _____ preserve me; for I wait on thee" (Psalms 25:21).
   e. "He that walketh in his _____ feareth the Lord: but he that is perverse in his ways despiseth him" (Proverbs 14:2).
   f. "Mark the perfect man, and behold the _____: for the end of that man is peace" (Psalms 37:37).

g. "The just man walketh in his integrity: his children are _____ after him" (Proverbs 20:7).

h. "I will praise thee with _____, when I shall have learned thy righteous judgments" (Psalms 119:7).

i. "If we say that we have fellowship with Him, and walk in darkness, we _____ and do not practice _____. But if we walk in the light as He is in the light, we have fellowship with one another, and the blood of Jesus Christ His Son cleanses us from all _____. If we say that we have no sin, we _____, and _____ is not in us. If we confess our sins, He is faithful and just to forgive us our sins and to cleanse us from all unrighteousness" (1 John 1:6-9).

j. "And this is the condemnation, that the light has come into the world, and men loved darkness rather than light, because their deeds were evil. For everyone practicing evil _____ the light and does not come to the light, lest his deeds should be _____. But he who does the truth _____, that his deeds may be clearly seen, that they have been done in God" (John 3:19-21).

k. "God is a Spirit: and they that _____ Him must worship Him in spirit and in _____" (John 4:24).

Truth is girded about the loins. The loins (Gk. *Osphus*) was the place where the Hebrews thought the generative power resided. This is why *osphus* is also translated as "descendants." You will _____ after your own kind. How you are and what you live by and teach is what others you mentor may believe and become (Proverbs 20:7).

2. ARMOR PIECE #2: THE BREASTPLATE OF RIGHTEOUSNESS

The Breastplate

The breastplate, or *lorica segmentata,* was a soldier's _____ for his chest and abdominal areas. Crafted of metal bands, the breastplate was sometimes called *"chainmail"* and it afforded critical protection from _____.

Before battle, a soldier would fasten the breastplate around his chest like a vest to protect his _____. If a soldier failed to wear his breastplate, an arrow could easily pierce his heart or lungs.

Every follower of Christ has a vital "spiritual organ" which needs to be guarded above all else. Proverbs 4:23 says, "Keep thy _____ with all diligence; for out of it are the issues of life." So critical is the condition of your spiritual heart that the Bible has nearly _____ verses referring to it. Many of those verses describe the kinds of hearts that please God: a _____ heart, a _____ heart, and a _____ heart. *"The sacrifices of God are a broken spirit: a broken and a contrite heart, O God, thou wilt not despise"* (Psalm 51:17).

God wants your "whole heart" and nothing less, for a heart sets the course of a person's life.

Jesus said that out of the abundance of the heart the _____ (Luke 6:45), and "where your _____ is, there will your heart be also" (Matthew 6:21). A heart that is not right toward God is like a "_____"(Psalm 78:57), like "a stubborn and rebellious generation; a generation that _____, and whose spirit was not _____ with God" (Psalm 78:8). If our heart is stubborn, hard, or proud, you will be unable to believe the Word of God.[1]

Why is your spiritual heart so important?
_____
_____

God offers us His righteousness on the basis of faith in His Son. *"Even the righteousness of God which is by faith of Jesus Christ unto all and upon all them that believe"* (Romans 3:22). None of us can earn right standing in God's eyes by following a list of rules, going to church, or doing good deeds. We are justified and made righteous only because of our _____ in the Lord Jesus. *"Not by the works of righteousness which we have done, but according to his mercy he saved us, by the washing of regeneration, and renewing of the Holy Ghost"* (Titus 3:5).

---

[1] Freely used by permission from Christ-centered Mall: www.ChristCenteredMall.com

Two key terms to remember as it pertains to the righteousness of God:

1. _____

   It is the legal act of God removing the guilt and penalty of sin while at the same time declaring a sinner righteous through Christ's atoning sacrifice.

2. _____

   "Christ is the end of the law for righteousness to everyone that believes" (Romans 10:4). *"For He hath made Him (Christ) to be _____, who knew no sin; that we might be the righteousness of God in Him"* (2 Corinthians 5:21).

The Fruit of Righteousness

Once we have received in our hearts the free gift of righteousness through faith in Jesus Christ, we have to allow His righteousness to begin to work on the inside of us and bear fruit. The bible speaks of "the fruit of righteousness." Philippians 1:11 says we are "_____ *with the fruits of righteousness* which are by Jesus Christ, unto the glory and praise of God."

   a. His Righteousness must be a _____ in our life. "Seek ye _____ the kingdom of God, and His _____; and all these things shall be added unto you" (Matthews 6:33). And "for the kingdom of God is not meat and drink; but righteousness, peace and joy IN the _____" (Romans 14:17). "_____ is the man who hungers and thirst for righteousness; for he shall be filled" (Matthews 5:6).

   b. Because of our long life lived in carnality, we are initially more prone to the sin nature living. Therefore, we have to be frequently _____ _____ (2 Timothy 3:16, 17). "All Scripture is given by inspiration of God, and is profitable for doctrine, for reproof, for correction, for _____, THAT the man of God may be complete, thoroughly equipped (furnished) unto all good works" (2 Timothy 3:16, 17).

   c. The fruit of righteousness is normally developed in us through not only the word of God but also through the _____ of the Lord (Hebrews 12:11).

d. If we are not chastened of the Lord then we are _____ (illegitimate) and not sons (Hebrews 12:8).

e. The Lord _____ us to live in His righteousness. "Who His own self bare our sins in His body on the tree, that we, being _____, *should live unto righteousness:* by whose stripes ye were healed" (2 Peter 2:24). Also Ephesians 4:24 tells us, "and that ye put on the new man, which after God is *created in righteousness* and true holiness."

f. Romans chapter Six illustrates that when we become "dead to sin" we are made "_____ to God." Romans 6:11-13, says, "Likewise you also, reckon yourselves to be dead indeed to sin, but alive to God IN Christ Jesus our Lord. Therefore DO NOT let sin _____ in your mortal body, that you should obey it in its lusts. And do not present your members as instruments of unrighteousness to sin, but present yourselves to God as being alive from the dead, and your members as *instruments of righteousness* to God."

g. The _____ flows heavier in your life when you are living in God's righteousness. "Thou hast _____ righteousness and hated iniquity; therefore God, even thy God, hast anointed thee with the oil of gladness above thy fellows" (Hebrews 1:9). This also speaks of God's favor toward you.

h. One thing that hinders the righteousness of God is _____. "For the wrath of man worketh not *the righteousness* of God" (James 1:20).

i. One secret to increasing the fruits of righteousness in your life is _____. "Now he that ministereth seed to the sower both ministers bread for your food, and multiply your seed sown and _____ *the fruits of your righteousness*" (2 Corinthians 9:10).

Conclusion: We must protect our most vital spiritual organ which is the heart, our innermost being, with the breastplate of righteousness. His righteousness is accredited unto us by His death on the cross and by faith we receive it and by faith we can allow it to bear fruit and give God glory and praise from a fruitful life of righteousness in Him. Thus, living in His righteousness becomes the protection we need for our hearts.

3. ARMOR PIECE #3: FEET SHOD WITH THE PREPARATION OF THE GOSPEL OF PEACE

Historical Background

No soldier can go far without the proper shoes. Even with all his other weapons, a barefoot soldier would soon become _____ by the rough terrain taking its toll on his feet. In Bible times, the breaking of a soldier's shoe was a metaphor for _____ or _____ (see Isaiah 5:27), signifying that a soldier's effectiveness was largely dependent upon his shoes.

A Roman soldier's caligae, or sandals, were constructed of leather and laced up the center of the foot and onto the ankle. At first glance, this kind of footwear might not appear to have afforded much protection, but the design was quite functional. The openness of the sandals enabled the soldier to wear them all day in his work, in marching, in fighting, and in standing for long periods of time — without getting blisters. The thick soles of the sandals were studded through with iron hobnails. These provided good traction and also came in handy when _____ the enemy.

Ephesians 6:15 describes a Christian's spiritual shoes as the "_____ of the gospel of peace."

The Feet

1. The feet are connected with what one uses to walk the _____.
2. Luke 1:79 – "To give light to those who sit in darkness and the shadow of death, to guide our feet into _____."
3. Romans 10:15 – "How beautiful are the _____ of those who preach the gospel of peace ..."
4. Hebrews 12:13 – "and make _____ paths for your feet, lest that which is lame be turned out of _____; but let it rather be _____. _____ peace with all men, and holiness, without no man shall see the Lord."
5. Matthew 3:3 – "Prepare the way of the LORD; Make His _____ straight."

Preparation (of the gospel of peace)

The word "Preparation" used here by Paul is the Greek word *"hetoimasia."*

Historically, the Hetoimasia or Etimasia _____
_____ is the Christian version of the symbolic subject of the _____ found in the art of the ancient world.

1. In Ancient Greece the empty throne represented _____, chief of the gods.
2. In early Buddhist art the empty throne represented _____.
3. In Early Christian art and Early Medieval art it is found in both the East and Western churches, and represents either _____, or sometimes God the Father as part of the Trinity.
4. In the Middle Byzantine period, from about 1000, it came to represent more specifically the throne prepared for the _____ of Christ, a meaning it has retained in Eastern Orthodox art to the present.
5. It carried the awareness and consciousness of _____.
6. For the later Byzantines the etimasia was _____ _____ of Matthew 24:30: "And then shall appear the sign of the Son of man in heaven: and then shall all the tribes of the earth mourn, and they shall see the Son of man coming in the clouds of heaven with power and great glory".

The understanding of the image as a symbol for the Second Coming also drew on Psalms 9:7: "But the Lord shall endure for ever: he hath _____," where the Septuagint has ("hetoimasen") for "prepared".

Psalm 89:14: "Justice and judgment are _____ of thy throne: mercy and truth shall go before thy face" is another relevant passage, using the word in the Septuagint (instead of the "habitation" of the King James Version), giving "preparation of your throne".

Throne imagery is found above all in the Book of Revelations, especially chapter 4, although the throne is already occupied.

To summarize, the preparation of the gospel of peace that Paul was signifying in Ephesians 6:15 is the kind of life preparation that one makes with the gospel of the Second Coming of Christ or Judgment seat of Christ in view. We also can use the term _____.

2 Timothy 2:21
"If a man therefore purge himself from these, he shall be a vessel unto _____, _____, and meet for the master's use, and _____ (hetoimazo) unto every good work."

1 Thessalonians 4:3, 4
"For this is _____, even your _____ that ye should abstain from fornication: that every one of you should know how to _____ in sanctification and honor."

2 Thessalonians 2:13
"But we are bound to give thanks always to God for you, brethren beloved of the Lord, because God hath from the beginning chosen you to salvation through _____ _____ and _____."

1 Peter 1:2
"Elect according to the foreknowledge of God the Father, through _____, unto obedience and sprinkling of the blood of Jesus Christ: Grace unto you, and peace, be multiplied."

Five facts about sanctification:

1. Sanctification is the _____ of allowing the holy character of God to be manifested in the _____ of regenerated men.[2]
2. Sanctification is the process of _____.
3. It is justification _____.
4. The enemy is fighting against your change, your transformation, your process, your development in God. He realizes that God justified you with a purpose and that purpose is to transform you to the image of His dear Son, Jesus

---

[2] http://www.christinyou.net/pages/sanoman.html ©1998 by James A. Fowler. All rights reserved.

Christ. Sanctification is the result of a _____ with God. It is _____ with the Spirit for your personal walk with God. It is allowing the Holy Spirit to work in you, "For it is God which _____ in you both to will and to do of His good pleasure (Philippians 2:13)."
5. We go through this process of change with the Second Coming of Christ in view.

Conclusion: We protect our feet (our spiritual walk) with the war sandals of sanctification, knowing that when Christ, who is our life shall appear, we shall appear with Him in glory (Colossians 3:4). This is the gospel of peace, that is, peace with God and the assurance that we shall be with Him in glory forever.

4. ARMOR PIECE #4: THE SHIELD OF FAITH

> "*Above all* taking the shield of faith, wherewith ye shall be able to quench all the fiery darts (flaming arrows) of the wicked" (Ephesians 6:16).

Faith is the shield of the Christian soldier, defending him from the _____ of the enemy from within and without.

The fiery darts are the _____ of the enemy.

The Shield

a. The shield of faith _____ the fiery darts (fierce attacks) of the wicked (enemy). To quench (Gk. *Sbennymi*) means to _____.
   Sbennymi is used metaphorically of suppressing _____.
b. The shield (Gk. *Thureos*) was a large oblong, four-cornered shield. It protected the _____. It kept the darts of the enemy away from the head, chest, waist, arms, and legs.
c. The shield also protects _____.
   When your shield is down, the other pieces of armor are exposed. Exposure of your armor gave the enemy confidence that he could find a way to take you out.

"Let us hold fast the profession of our faith without wavering; (for he is faithful that promised)" (Hebrews 10:23).

d. The shield _____. A skilled soldier can use the shield to hold back the darts of the enemy no matter the direction they come from.[3]

e. "_____ Abraham; for I am thy shield and exceeding great reward" (Genesis 15:1).

f. "The Lord is my strength and my shield; my heart _____ in Him, and I am helped" (Psalms 28:7).

g. "Our soul _____ for the Lord: He is our help and our shield" (Psalms 33:20).

h. "For the Lord God is a sun and shield: the Lord will give grace and glory: no good thing will He withhold from them that _____" (Psalms 84:11).

i. "Every word of God is pure: He is a shield unto them that put their _____ in Him" (Proverbs 30:5).

j. "For thou, Lord, wilt bless _____; with _____ wilt thou compass him as with a shield" (Psalms 5:12).

Faith

a. "Now faith is the _____ of things hoped for (Gk. *Elpis [Elpizo] expected; cheerfully anticipated);* the _____ of things not seen" (Hebrews 11:1).

b. Faith is the substance. The Greek word used for substance is hypostasis which means _____

c. Faith is confidence or assurance in things we _____.

d. What are the things that the Christians suppose to cheerfully anticipate?
_____
_____

e. "And everyone that has this hope will _____ even as He is pure" (1 John 3:3).

f. "But _____ the Lord God in your hearts: and be ready always to give an answer to every man that asketh you a reason of the hope that is in you with meekness and fear" (1 Peter 3:15).

---

3   http://www.wordlibrary.co.uk/article.php?id=97

g. "Blessed be the God and Father of our Lord Jesus Christ, which according to his abundant mercy hath begotten us again unto _____ *(active, energetic, vivacious, spirited, full of life)* hope by the resurrection of Jesus Christ from the dead" (1 Peter 1:3).

h. "Looking for the _____, and the glorious appearing of the great God and our Savior Jesus Christ" (Titus 2:13).

i. "Believe on Me as the Scriptures has said, then out of your innermost being (belly) shall flow rivers of living waters. This He spake concerning the _____ (John 7:37, 38). If you have a lively hope you'll have a flowing river!

j. "Faith comes by _____ and hearing by the word of God" (Romans 10:17).

k. "Building up your most holy faith _____" (Jude 1:21).

l. "For it is by _____ that ye are saved through faith" (Ephesians 2:8).

m. "By whom we have _____ by faith into this grace wherein we stand" (Romans 5:2). Faith is what God has given us to _____ from Him. He designed it that way. For He is the author and the finisher of our faith.

n. The Four C's of Faith

   i. _____: "The state or appearance of being _____; persuasion." "And being fully persuaded that, what he had promised, he was able also to perform" (Romans 4:21). "Let every man be fully persuaded in his own mind" (Romans 14:5).

   ii. _____: full trust (reliance or dependence); belief (assurance) in the power, trustworthiness, or reliability of a person (in this case, God).

   iii. _____: Engagement or involvement. The World English Dictionary defines commitment as an obligation, promise that _____ _____. *Commitment is a very important character trait to have. It means *to be responsible, having devotion and never giving up, staying the course in spite of the challenges.* It also means *"to be honest and true to the task or journey of which you have agreed to embark."*[4] Paul told Timothy, "For I know whom I have believed, and *am persuaded* that he is able to keep that which *I have committed* unto him against that day" (2 Timothy 1:12).

---

[4] www.reference.com/motif/health/quotes-on-commitment

iv. _____: This means _____; declaring the word of God and His promises. "These all died in faith, not having received the promises [in their lifetime], but having seen them afar off, and were persuaded of them, and embraced them, and *confessed* that they were strangers and pilgrims on the earth" (Hebrews 11:13).

5. ARMOR PIECE #5: THE SWORD OF THE SPIRIT

Ephesians 6:17
"And the sword of the Spirit, which is the _____ of God."

Historical Background

The Roman sword, or *gladius,* was crafted of iron. Blacksmiths hardened the iron by coating the red-hot sword blade with coal dust, thus forming a hard carbon coating on the blade. Sword handles were made of iron, ivory, bone, or wood.

The Romans used their swords both _____ and _____.

Used in a defensive manner, the sword, along with the other armor pieces, enabled the soldier to _____ the enemy's blows.

As an offensive weapon, the sword was used to _____ and counter-attack an enemy until the weapon seriously wounded or killed the assailant. In battle, rows of Roman soldiers pressed back their enemies one step at a time by alternating a forward thrust of the shield (_____) with a forward plunge of the sword (_____).[5]

Biblical Parallels

There are two Greek words for the word, "Word." They are _____ and _____. They are similar in meaning.

---

[5] www.christcenteredmall.com/teachings/armor-of-god-7.htm

They both mean "that which is or has been uttered by the living _____, embodying a conception or idea. Any sound produced by the voice that has definite _____. A declaration of one's _____ made in words."

Logos

John 1:1-4, 14

"In the beginning was the Word (logos), and the Word (logos) was with God, and the Word (logos) was God. The same was in the beginning with God. All things were made by Him; and without Him was not anything made that was made. In Him was life and the life was the light of men… And the Word was made flesh, and dwelt among us, and we beheld His glory, the glory as of the only begotten of the Father, full of grace and truth."

Jesus is the logos of God, the incarnate Word. Jesus is the embodiment of everything God has ever spoken or ever will speak.

Rhema

Rhema is a tailor-made word cut out and designed for the specificity of your needs. It's a living, active, relevant word, i.e. a *"right now word."* There is no rhema word (revelation, prophetic word) that is unaligned or misaligned with the Logos of God (written word of God that points to Christ). Rhema is the logos coming to life for you. Rhema comes forth from Logos. It's when the Holy Spirit _____ or _____ your heart and mind making His written word alive and relative to your present situation. It becomes personal to you. It must be mixed with _____ in order for you to profit or benefit from it (Hebrews 4:2).

Hebrews 4:12

"For the *word of God* is _____, and _____, and _____ _____, piercing even to the dividing asunder of soul and spirit, and of the joints and marrow, and is a _____ of the *thoughts and intents of the heart.*"

Romans 10:17
"So then faith cometh by hearing, and hearing by _____ of God."

Matthews 4:4
"But he answered and said, It is written, Man shall not live by bread alone, but *by every word* that _____ out of the mouth of God."

Matthews 18:16
"But if he will not hear thee, then take with thee one or two more, that in the mouth of two or three witnesses every word may be _____."

Mark 14:72
"And the second time the cock crew. And Peter _____ the word that Jesus said unto him, Before the cock crow twice, thou shalt deny me thrice. And when he thought thereon, he wept."

Luke 1:37-38
"For with God _____ (lit. *"no rhema"* or *"no word"*) shall be impossible. And Mary said, "Behold the handmaid of the Lord; be it unto me _____. And the angel departed from her."

John 6:63
It is the spirit that _____; the flesh profiteth nothing: the words that I speak unto you, they are _____, and they are _____.

John 8:47
He that is of God _____ God's words: ye therefore hear them not, because ye are not of God.

John 14:10
Believest thou not that I am in the Father, and the Father in me? The words that I speak unto you I speak not of myself: but the Father that dwelleth in me, he _____.

John 15:7
If ye _____ in me, and my _____ abide in you, ye shall ask what ye will, and it shall be done unto you.

Acts 10:44
While Peter yet spake these words, the Holy Ghost fell on all them which _____ the word.

Ephesians 5:26
That he might _____ and _____ it [the church] with the washing of the water by the word.

Hebrews 11:3
Through faith we understand that *the worlds were framed by the word of God,* so that _____ were not made of things which do appear.

Hebrews 4:1
Let us therefore fear, lest, a promise being left us of entering into his rest, any of you should seem to come short of it. For unto us was the gospel preached, as well as unto them: but the word preached did not profit them, not being _____ in them that heard it.

The apostle John had a vision of Jesus while imprisoned on the isle of Patmos. John described the Lord as having a "sharp two-edged sword" coming out of His mouth (Revelation 1:16). Later, John wrote, "And I saw heaven opened, and behold a white horse; and he that sat upon him was called Faithful and True, and in righteousness he doth judge and make war ... and his name is called _____ ...out of his mouth goeth a _____, that with it he should smite the nations: and he shall rule them with a rod of iron" (Revelation 19:11-16).

Jesus, Who is the Word (John 1:1, 14), has graciously given us His written Word, the Bible. The written Word (all Scripture) was given to men by inspiration of God, and it is profitable for _____, for _____, for _____, and for _____ (II Timothy 3:16-17; II Peter 1:21).

The Word is made alive by the Holy Spirit of God, causing it to be filled with divine energy and ability. "So shall my word be that goeth forth out of my mouth: it shall not return unto me void, but _____

_____" (Isaiah 55:11).

God's Word, our sword of the Spirit, is able to cut down the strongholds of Satan. Tragically, however, many Christians fail to wield their swords. Instead, they display their swords as a decorative shelf piece: beautiful to look at, but of little practical use. This passive approach merely gives the enemy a greater advantage. The Lord said to Israel's leader Joshua, "This book of the law (the written word) shall not depart out of _____; but thou shalt _____ therein day and night, that thou mayest _____ according to all that is written therein" (Joshua 1:8-9; also see Psalms 1:2, 119:97-100). By _____ using the word of God, Joshua would have a huge advantage over his enemies: his way would be _____ and _____ and the Lord promised to go with him wherever he went.

Conclusion: Learning to use the sword of God's Word requires many hours of practice. Don't wait until the heat of battle to learn to use your sword! Rather, store up Scripture in your mind and heart on a regular basis through *memorization* and *meditation*. What do those words mean? Memorization means to commit a passage to memory, while meditation means *to thoroughly process, ponder, think about, and apply a passage of Scripture.* II Timothy 2:15 says, "_____ to shew thyself approved unto God, a workman that needeth not to be ashamed, rightly dividing the word of truth."

The more you memorize and meditate upon God's Word, the more natural it will become to wield the sword. You will gain confidence in speaking the Word, praying the Word, and singing the Word. The Scriptures you hide in your heart and apply to your life will be with you at all times, even if your Bible isn't nearby. "Thy word is a lamp unto my feet and a light unto my path" (Psalm 119:105).

Remember that the sword is both an offensive and a defensive weapon. Used offensively, you hide God's Word in your heart, root out sin, and strengthen your inner man with God's promises before the enemy attacks. Used defensively, you deflect the devil's lies, doubts, and temptations with the truth of the Word. As you learn to effectively use your sword against the wiles of the enemy, remember the Lord's words to you: "Fear thou not; for I am with thee: be not dismayed; for I am thy God: I will strengthen thee; yea, I will help thee; yea, I will uphold thee with the right hand of my righteousness" (Isaiah 41:10).

6. ARMOR PIECE #6: HELMET OF SALVATION

Historical Background

A Roman soldier's helmet, known as the *cassis* or *galea,* protected a soldier's skull and neck from enemy blows and falling debris. Fashioned from bronze or iron, the helmet included two hinged side pieces to protect the cheekbones and jaw. Helmets were often lined inside with sponge or felt for the sake of comfort.

Horsehair plumes frequently adorned the tops of soldiers' helmets. Although not used in battle, these plumes were dyed a variety of colors to distinguish the rank of military officers and were primarily used for ceremonial purposes.

Salvation

What does salvation mean to you?
_____
_____

Of the many Hebrew words used to signify salvation, *yasa* appears most frequently in the Old Testament. Yasa means _____
_____. Commonly, the deliverance of which the Old Testament speaks is physical in nature, though there are important exceptions. In contrast, the employment of _____ in the New Testament, though it may include physical deliverance and material preservation, usually signifies _____
_____. In addition to the notion of deliverance, the Bible also uses salvation to denote _____
_____.

Seven things believers of Christ are promised to be delivered from:

1. _____
2. _____
3. _____
4. _____
5. _____
6. _____
7. _____

Scriptures on Salvation

Moses, when escaping from Egyptian bondage, came nigh unto the Red Sea and seeing a swift pace Army approaching him and the people of Israel to destroy them, lifted up his rod and declared, "Fear ye not, stand still and see the _____ of the Lord" (Exodus 14:13).

Psalms 21:1, 5

The king shall joy in _____, O LORD; and in thy salvation how greatly shall he rejoice! His _____ is great in thy salvation: honour and majesty hast thou laid upon him.

Psalms 27:1

The LORD is my light and my salvation; whom shall I fear? The LORD is the _____; of whom shall I be afraid?

Psalms 35:3, 9

Draw out also the spear, and stop the way against them that persecute me: say unto my soul, I am thy salvation. And my soul shall be joyful in the LORD: it shall rejoice in his salvation.

Psalms 51:12

Restore unto me _____ of thy salvation; and uphold me with thy free spirit.

Psalms 53:6
Oh that the salvation of Israel were come out of Zion! When God bringeth back the captivity of his people, Jacob shall _____, and Israel shall be glad.

Isaiah 12:2-3
Behold, God is my salvation; I will trust, and not be afraid: for the LORD JEHOVAH is my strength and my song; he also is become my salvation. Therefore with joy shall ye draw water out of the wells of salvation.

Acts 4:12
Neither is there salvation in any other: for there is _____ under heaven given among men, whereby we must be saved.

Romans 1:16
For I am not ashamed of _____: for it is _____ _____ to everyone that believeth; to the Jew first, and also to the Greek. (also 2 Timothy 3:15 - And that from a child thou hast known the holy scriptures, which are able to make thee _____ through faith which is in Christ Jesus)

Romans 10:10
For with the heart man believeth unto righteousness; and with the mouth _____ is made unto salvation.

Romans 13:11
And that, knowing the time, that now it is high time to awake out of sleep: for now is our salvation _____ than when we believed.

2 Corinthians 7:10
For _____ worketh repentance to salvation not to be repented of: but the sorrow of the world worketh death.

Philippians 2:12
Wherefore, my beloved, as ye have always obeyed, not as in my presence only, but now much more in my absence, _____ your own salvation with fear and trembling.

1 Thessalonians 5:8-9
But let us, who are of the day, be _____, putting on the breastplate of faith and love; and for an helmet, the hope of salvation. For God hath not appointed us to _____, but to obtain salvation by our Lord Jesus Christ.

2 Thessalonians 2:13
God hath from the beginning chosen you to salvation through _____ of the Spirit and _____ of the truth:

Titus 2:11-14
For the grace of God that bringeth salvation hath appeared to all men, _____ that, denying ungodliness and worldly lusts, we should live soberly, righteously, and godly, in this present world; Looking for that blessed hope, and the glorious appearing of the great God and our Saviour Jesus Christ; Who gave himself for us, that he might redeem us from all iniquity, and purify unto himself a peculiar people, zealous of good works.

Hebrews 6:9
But, beloved, we are persuaded _____ of you, and things that _____ salvation, though we thus speak.

The Mind

> "O God the Lord, the strength of my salvation,
> thou hast *covered my head* in the day of battle" (Psalm 140:7).

The helmet of salvation covers the mind. Many of Satan's battles against us happen in the mind. The devil can flash evil and lewd _____ into our minds hoping that we will entertain his thoughts and _____ (James 1:13-15).

Satan can also bombard our thoughts with _____, hoping to carve away at our _____ in the Lord and get us _____.

But perhaps the devil's most subtle strategy is mind manipulation through subliminal messaging. Make no mistake, Satan is the god of this world, and he aims to keep people focused on the things of this world. He influences news media, advertisements, and popular music (even so-called gospel music) to condition people to accept the "values" of his anti-God, man-centered world system. "But I fear, lest by any means, as the serpent beguiled Eve through his subtlety, so your minds should be _____ from the _____ that is in Christ" (II Corinthians 11:3; also see 4:4).

1. **Corrupt**: Gk. *Phtheiros* – means _____
    a. In the opinion of the Jews, the temple was corrupted or "destroyed" when anyone defiled or in the slightest degree damaged anything in it, or if its guardians _____ their duties.
    a. To _____ a Christian church from that state of knowledge and holiness in which it ought to abide
2. **Simplicity**: Gk. *Haplotes* – means singleness, sincerity, _____ _____, the virtue of one who is free from pretence and hypocrisy. Not self seeking, openness of heart manifesting itself by generosity

Romans 12:1-2

I beseech you therefore, brethren, *by the mercies of God,* that ye present your bodies a living sacrifice, holy, acceptable unto God, which is your reasonable service. And be not conformed to this world: but be ye transformed by the _____, that ye may prove what is that good, and acceptable, and perfect, will of God.

Conclusion: The helmet of salvation protects us from mental corruption or mental destruction and keeps us mentally honest and single-minded which is focused on our relationship with Jesus Christ and how we ought to please Him.

The helmet of salvation helps guard us from doubt, fear, inward and outward lies, lewdness and evil thoughts from the media, music, entertainment, schools, or any other man-centered systems that defy the faith. We must contend for the faith that was delivered unto us (Jude 1:3), because we have been privileged to have such a great salvation (Hebrews 2:3).

Spiritual Warfare—Defeat Your Enemy and Live a Victorious Life

THE SWORD OF THE SPIRIT WHICH IS THE WORD OF GOD

LESSON 5

HOW TO DEFEAT THE ENEMY (PART II): THE WEAPONS OF OUR WARFARE

We are in a daily spiritual battle against the enemy of our soul. Fortunately, our God has equipped us with weapons for this warfare. We have to go to our kingdom armory and sign out our weapons that will enable us to defeat our enemy daily. The weaponry that we have are mighty through God and will allow us to bring destruction upon the stratagems of the enemy. God's mighty weaponry and what they can do for us is found in 2 Corinthians 10:3-6. Here are six different Bible versions on 2 Corinthians 10:3-6:

King James Version
"For though we walk in the flesh, we do not war after the flesh: (For the weapons of our warfare are not _____, but mighty through God to the pulling down of _____, casting down _____, and every _____ that exalteth itself _____, and bringing into captivity every thought to the _____ of Christ; and having in a _____ all disobedience, when your obedience is fulfilled."

The Complete Jewish Bible
"For although we do live in the world, we do not wage war in a worldly way; because the weapons we use to wage war are not _____. On the contrary, they have God's power for _____ strongholds. We demolish _____ and every _____ that raises itself up against the knowledge of God; we take every thought captive and _____ the Messiah. And when you have become _____ obedient, then we will be ready to punish every act of disobedience."

The New American Standard Bible (NASB)

"For though we walk in the flesh, we do not war according to the flesh, for the weapons of our warfare are not of the flesh, but divinely powerful for the _____. We are destroying _____ and every lofty thing raised up against the knowledge of God, and we are taking every thought captive to the obedience of Christ, and we are ready to punish all disobedience, whenever your obedience is complete."

The Amplified Bible (AMP)

"For though we walk (live) in the flesh, we are not carrying on our warfare according to the flesh and using _____ weapons. For the weapons of our warfare are not _____ [weapons of flesh and blood], but they are mighty before God for the _____ and destruction of strongholds, [Inasmuch as we] _____ arguments and _____ and _____ and every _____ and lofty thing that sets itself up against the [true] knowledge of God; and we lead every thought and _____ away captive into the obedience of Christ (the Messiah, the Anointed One), Being in readiness to punish every [insubordinate for his] disobedience, when your own _____ _and obedience [as a church] are fully secured and complete."

The New International Version (NIV)

"For though we live in the world, we do not wage war as the world does. The weapons we fight with are not the weapons of the world. On the contrary, they have divine power to demolish strongholds. We demolish arguments and every _____ that sets itself up against the knowledge of God, and we take captive every thought to make it obedient to Christ. And we will be ready to punish every act of disobedience, once your obedience is complete."

The New Living Translation (NLT)

"We are human, but we don't wage war with human _____ and _____. We use God's mighty weapons, not mere worldly weapons, to knock down the strongholds of human reasoning and to destroy false arguments. With these weapons we break down every proud argument that _____. With these weapons we conquer their _____, and we teach them to obey Christ. And we will punish those who remained disobedient after the rest of you became loyal and obedient."

The Warfare

a. _____.

The enemy is doing all he can to destroy the purposes of God on the earth for mankind. Many believers do absolutely nothing to fight back against the wicked campaign of Satan.

b. _____.

God has fully equipped us with His divine weaponry to engage the enemy in battle and for us to come out victorious.

   i. "Fight the good fight of faith, lay hold on eternal life, whereunto thou art also called, and hast professed a good profession before many witnesses." (1 Timothy 6:12).

   ii. "I have fought a good fight, I have finished my course, I have kept the faith" (2 Timothy 4:6).

c. _____.

   i. "Thou therefore _____, as a _____ soldier of Jesus Christ. No man that warreth entangleth himself with the affairs of this life; that he may _____ him who hath chosen him to be a soldier" (2 Timothy 2:3-4).

   ii. 2 Timothy 2:4 NASB – "No soldier in active service entangles himself in the affairs of everyday life, so that he may please the one who enlisted him as a soldier."

d. As a good soldier we are to _____ _____. What is a "hardship?" _____
_____

List some words used in Scripture that are synonymous with "hardship."

1. _____
2. _____
3. _____
4. _____
5. We should have a _____ and _____ not dereliction to duty. Our aim is _____ who enlisted us.
6. We have a method. The Bible says, "The weapons of _____." The

word *"warfare"* is the Greek word *"strateia"* which means _____
_____
_____. It is where we get our English
word _____, which means "_____
_____." God gives us His strategy and plan in fighting the enemy.
  a. This strategy is not carnal, natural or physical. Only God's strategy and not mere human plans can disrupt and defeat any satanic opposition.
  b. We fight with divinely powerful weapons that come from _____. List some of the weapons that God has given us to defeat the enemy:
     iii. _____
     iv. _____
     v. _____
     vi. _____
     vii. _____
     viii. _____
     ix. _____
     x. _____
     xi. _____
     xii. _____

These divinely powerful weapons that we receive from God enable us to destroy (demolish) strongholds.

In your own words, what do you think Paul meant by "stronghold?"
_____
_____
_____

The Greek word used for stronghold is "ochuroma" and it means _____
_____.
It is a place that conceals people from coming into it. It is used figuratively of a _____ in which a person seeks _____.

Note: Arguments are disagreements in which different views are expressed, often angrily. They are debates whether something is correct.

In 2 Corinthians 10:3-6, apostle Paul considered four things to be strongholds. These four things are:

1. _____
2. _____
3. _____
4. _____

IMAGINATIONS

What do you feel is implied in this verse when it uses the word "imaginations?"

_____
_____
_____
_____
_____
_____

The New Testament word used for "imaginations" here in 2 Corinthians 10:5 is "logismos." It is where we get our English word "logic." Logismos means:

_____
_____
_____
_____
_____
_____

1. _____ are opinions, conclusions or theories based on incomplete or incorrect facts or information.
2. _____ is the use of logical thinking in order to find results or draw conclusions.

3. _____ is the result of a calculation. When you gather your information and thoughts and you come to a final conclusion or decision. It is the collection of thoughts which forms a decisive opinion. (Mind made up!)

Strongholds are speculations, opinions and conclusions drawn on incomplete or incorrect facts. Strongholds are incorrect judgments that were given about you (from other people or even from your own conscience about yourself). A stronghold is logical thinking that is hostile to faith in Christ or you exercising faith to produce God-intended results.

The root word for imagination is *image*. Image is important to God. In fact, he created us in His image. The dictionary definition for image is *"a picture in your mind or an idea of how someone or something is. It is a mind-picture or idea that forms in a reader's or listener's mind from the words that they read or hear."* When people see the believers they should see a reflection of the character of our heavenly Father and can imagine their lives being in right relationship with him as well. This is one of the reasons why Jesus came, i.e., to show us what the Father was like. Hebrews 1:3 says that Yeshua was *"the express image of His person."* Now, all believers are reconciled to the Father through Christ and are commanded to be conformed to the image of His dear Son (Yeshua). We can walk like Yeshua walked on the earth. We can truly be Christ-like.

In Noah's generation, men went after the evil imaginations of their hearts.

Genesis 6:5

"And God saw that the wickedness of man was great in the earth, and that every imagination of the thoughts of his heart was only evil continually."

The word used in this verse for imagination is yetser which initially means "to form, frame or a thing worked, as in pottery, a graven image or even man as formed from the dust. This gave the greater meaning of what goes on in a person's heart and therefore became interpreted as "purpose or intent."

There are two kinds of imaginations (heart purposes and intents—mental pictures that frame the reason why a person committed a certain act, i.e., they deviced a plan to do something):

1. evil imagination
2. good or holy imagination

What spiritual disciplines help us cultivate holy imaginations and a healthy, pure heart?

1. _____   3. _____
2. _____   4. _____

Hebrews 4:12

"For the word of God is quick, and powerful, and sharper than any twoedged sword, piercing even to the dividing asunder of soul and spirit, and of the joints and marrow, and is a discerner of the thoughts and *intents of the heart*."

In the Tanakh (Old Testament), physical statues were erected to represent different deities (gods) of worship; sometimes they were called groves, idols or _____ (*graven images*). Worship of these statues usually invoked the presence of a spirit (demon).

Exodus 34:11-14

"Observe thou that which I command thee this day: behold, I drive out before thee the Amorite, and the Canaanite, and the Hittite, and the Perizzite, and the Hivite, and the Jebusite. Take heed to thyself, lest thou make a covenant with the inhabitants of the land whither thou goest, lest it be for a snare in the midst of thee: But ye shall *destroy their <u>altars</u> (for worship and sacrificing), break their <u>images (sacred pillars, monuments)</u>, and cut down their <u>groves</u> (<u>Asherim</u> - plural form of Asherah/Astarte [Easter] (where Hadassah was renamed by the Persians, Esther); she was the goddess of fortune and happiness)*: <u>For thou shalt worship no other god: for the Lord, whose name is Jealous, is a jealous God.</u>"

There were two purposes for these graven images:
1. To invoke a deity
2. To mark territories for people to see and recognize the gods that were served in that particular land or nation and to demand paying homage to it

King Manasseh's sin:

2 Kings 21:17 - Now the rest of the acts of Manasseh, and all that he did, and <u>his sin that he sinned</u>, are they not written in the book of the chronicles of the kings of Judah?

2 Kings 21:2-7, 11

And he did that which was evil in the sight of the Lord, after the abominations of the heathen, whom the Lord cast out before the children of Israel. For he built up again the high places which Hezekiah his father had destroyed; and he reared up altars for Baal, and made a grove, as did Ahab king of Israel; and worshipped all the host of heaven, and served them. And he built altars in the house of the Lord, of which the Lord said, In Jerusalem will I put my name. And he built altars for all the host of heaven in the two courts of the house of the Lord. And he made his son pass through the fire, and observed times, and used enchantments, and dealt with familiar spirits and wizards: he wrought much wickedness in the sight of the Lord, to provoke him to anger. And he set a graven image of the grove that he had made in the house, of which the Lord said to David, and to Solomon his son, In this house, and in Jerusalem, which I have chosen out of all tribes of Israel, will I put my name for ever... Because Manasseh king of Judah hath done these abominations, and hath done wickedly above all that the Amorites did, which were before him, and hath made Judah also to sin with his idols:

King Manasseh committed 10 sins when he decided to go after the abominations of the heathens *(nations who did not serve Yahweh)* by:

1. <u>Built up the high places that King Hezekiah destroyed</u>
2. <u>Reared up altars for the god *Baal*</u>
3. <u>Made a grove</u>
4. <u>Worshipped all the host of heaven (and served them)</u>
5. <u>Built altars in the house of the Lord where the Lord's name, *Yahweh* (YHWH) was to be established in Jerusalem forever</u>
6. <u>Made his son pass through the fire</u>
7. <u>Observed times</u>
8. <u>Used enchantments</u>

9. Dealt with familiar spirits and wizards
10. Made Judah also to sin with his idols

When observing the 10 commandments which was Yahweh's covenant with his people, King Manasseh's sin was breaking (obliterating) the first commandment—he served other gods by erecting restoring demonic high places, altars and groves and ultimately encouraging the southern kingdom of Judah to sin along with him. His very name, Manasseh, means "to cause to forget." The purpose of these images is to cause people to forget Yahweh. The more of these images and sacred pillars were built, the easier it was for people to pay attention to them and not observe Yahweh and his commandments.

What are some images erected in today's society that the enemy has set up in the world that causes people to forget God?

_____
_____
_____
_____

HIGH THINGS

What do you think Paul meant by *"high things"* that rises up against the knowledge of God? And what did he mean by the "knowledge of God?"

_____
_____
_____
_____
_____

The Greek word for "high thing" is hypsoma which means "an elevated thing or height. It can mean an elevated structure, i.e., a barrier, bulward, wall, rampart, etc.

_____ are high things. To make an excuse means to justify something. It is an explanation not necessarily true, given in order to make something appear more acceptable or less offensive. An excuse is a false reason that enables somebody to do something he or she wants to do.

Excuses are strongholds that protect people from receiving the plan of God for their life. You can explain yourself out of God's grace, plan and will for your life.

Excuses are lies you tell yourself (or someone else tells you) that convince you to reject the saving knowledge of Yeshua haMashiach (Jesus Christ). These excuses can be religious lies and beliefs embedded in the heart like Islam, Hinduism, reincarnation, etc.

These excuses can be misleading ungodly values about marriage, money and social tolerances like drgus and alcohol, certain kinds of music, etc.

The Lord has given us weapons that can destroy excuses and lies built up in our minds.

THOUGHTS

Apostle Paul uses the word "noema" for "thoughts" here in 2 Corinthians 10:5. This word means *"a mental perception; an evil purpose: device (a ploy or way of achieving soemthing in a dishonest way)."* It can also mean *"a secret plot."* They are plans that are contrary to the plan of God for your life. There are people that Satan has employed to plot evil against you, to bring you down and ruin you and hinder the promises of God from coming to pass in your life.

What is the significance of *thoughts* as being a "stronghold?"

_____
_____
_____
_____
_____

These thoughts or secret plots have to be brought into captivity, arrested and bound up by the power of Jesus' name in order for us to walk in obedience to God's will. Do the things you are planning line up with the will of God?

DISOBEDIENCE

What does disobedience mean to you?

_____

_____

Cambridge dictionary defines disobedience as refusing to do what someone in authority tells you to do. Disobedience is a stronghold that makes you _____. It is the pursuit of the ungodly plans and schemes that you desire.

The late Dr. Myles Munroe once said, "_____
_____.
Success alone is not enough; you must succeed in the right thing. Sincerity alone is not enough because you can be sincerely wrong. Faithfulness alone is not enough because you can faithful to the wrong faith. Commitment alone is not enough because you can be committed to the wrong cause. Succeeding in the wrong assignment is failure."[1]

Disobedience is pursuing the wrong assignment while _____ the leading of the Holy Spirit. Proverbs 19:21 says, "many are the plans in a person's heart, but it is the Lord's purpose that prevails."

Our greatest desire should be to fulfill the purposes of God for our lives. Let His purpose conquer all other plans that come to our minds that our only action should be the will of God. If we settle for anything less it is to us _____.

A READINESS to Revenge all Disobedience

2 Corinthians 10:6 says we must have a *"readiness"* to revenge all disobedience when our obedience is fulfilled. This means we should be _____ to dissuade ourselves from acting rebelliously against the Holy Spirit's leading. When we recognize ourselves acting contrary to the influence of the voice of Yah, we should be ready to _____ those actions. Disobedience should never be acceptable or tolerated. God wants your absolute obedience.

---

1   Dr. Myles Munroe, Applying the Kingdom, Destiny Image Publishers, Inc., P.O. Box 310, Shippensburg, PA 17257-0310, pp. 15-16

OBEDIENCE

The goal of spiritual warfare is obedience. We struggle and fight an enemy who does not want us to obey God. It was becasue of Adam's disobedience that sin and death entered the world. Mankind was separated from God because of his disobedience to the commandments given to him in the garden of Eden. Disobedience is still at work in mankind today (Ephesians 2:2). God's wrath will come upon the children of disobedience (Ephesians 5:6, Colossians 3:6). The only way to a life of obedience to God is through faith in his Son, Yeshua haMashiach (Jesus Christ).

Romans 5:19

> For as by one man's disobedience many were made sinners, so by the obedience of one shall many be made righteous.

Deuteronomy 28:1, 2

"And it shall come to pass, if thou shalt *hearken diligently* unto the voice of the Lord thy God, to observe and to do all his commandments which I command thee this day, that the Lord thy God will set thee on high above all nations of the earth: And all these blessings shall come on thee, and overtake thee, if thou shalt hearken unto the voice of the Lord thy God."

The Lord promised to bless his people in such a way that will elevate them above all other nations (Deuteronomy 28:1-14). But the blessings were contingent upon their obedience to his voice, which was observing and following his commandments.

Moses, who was known to be the author of Deuteronomy, uses an interesting Hebrew phrase that was translated in English as *"hearken diligently."* He uses the same Hebrew word twice. He says, *"Shama shama."*

Shama means "to hear intelligently and attentively and respond appropriately." Obedience is appropriately responding to what you hear with a focused ear.

Shama shama is diligently obeying, hearing intensely. So, not only are you focused on what the Lord is speaking, but you have a determination, a passion to respond faithfully to him. It's hearing on purpose. You purposed to do his will. You can't wait to hear what he says so that you can act upon it. How do you demonstrate to Yah that you are passionate about what he has to say?

_____
_____
_____
_____
_____

With this kind of heart posture, the Lord can't do anything but perform his good will toward you and bless you bountifully. It is so important to train your ear to hear the Holy Spirit's voice. Yeshua says, "My sheep hear my voice, and I know them, and they follow me" (John 10:27).

Genesis 22:18
"In your seed all the nations of the earth shall be blessed, because you have obeyed My voice."

Hebrews 11:8
"By faith Abraham, when he was called to go out into a place which he should after receive for an inheritance, obeyed; and he went out, not knowing whither he went."

Conclusion: Our fight is against a real enemy who has built up strongholds in men's hearts and minds (including our own) in an attempt to cause us to resist the reality of God and the need for a Savior, which is Yeshua (Jesus Christ) alone. These strongholds are intellectual arguments and rebellious excuses and proud and vain imaginations that harden the heart of man and keep him alienated from the life of God. Only the mighty supernatural weapons of God can deliver man from his own depravity and destruction caused by Satan's deceit. <u>With the whole armor of God and the weapons of our warfare we can live in complete victory and cripple the kingdom of darkness and bring many souls to Christ.</u> Let us please the One who has enlisted us into His army and become good soldiers of the cross and cause of Christ. *Obedience is better than sacrifice.*

THE SHIELD OF FAITH

LESSON 6
REWARDS FOR OVERCOMERS

Romans 8:36-39

"Who shall separate us from the love of Christ? shall tribulation, or distress, or persecution, or famine, or nakedness, or peril, or sword? As it is written, For thy sake we are killed all the day long; we are accounted as sheep for the slaughter. Nay, in all these things <u>we are more than conquerors through him that loved us.</u> For I am persuaded, that neither death, nor life, nor angels, nor principalities, nor powers, nor things present, nor things to come, Nor height, nor depth, nor any other creature, shall be able to separate us from the love of God, which is in Christ Jesus our Lord."

1 John 5:4

"For whatsoever is born of God <u>overcometh the world</u>: and this is the victory that overcometh the world, even our faith."

1. DEFINITION OF AN OVERCOMER

Overcomers are followers of Christ who successfully _____ the power and _____ of the world's system. An overcomer holds fast to faith in Christ until the end. He does not turn away when times get difficult or become an apostate. Overcoming requires complete dependence upon God for direction, purpose, fulfillment, and strength to follow His plan for our lives (Proverbs 3:5–6; 2 Corinthians 12:9).

The Greek word most often translated "overcomer" stems from the word *nike* which, according to Strong's Concordance, means "_____." The verb implies *a battle*." The Bible teaches believers to recognize that the world is a battleground, not a _____.

An overcomer is one who _____ temptation no matter what lures Satan uses.

The apostle Paul wrote eloquently of overcoming in Romans 8:35–39. He summarizes the power believers have through the Holy Spirit to overcome any attacks of the enemy. Verse 37 says, "In all these things we are *more than conquerors* through him who loved us."

Overcoming is often equated with _____. Yeshua encouraged those who followed Him to _____ (Matthew 24:13). A true disciple of Christ is one who endures through trials by the power of the Holy Spirit. An overcomer clings to Christ, no matter how high the cost of discipleship. Hebrews 3:14 says, "We have come to share in Christ, if indeed we hold our original conviction _____ to the very end."

In the book of Revelation, Yeshua promised great rewards to those who overcome. Yeshua warned that holding fast to Him would not be easy, but it would be well worth it. In Mark 13:13, He says, "You _____ by all for my name's sake. But the one who endures to the end will be saved" (ESV). We have the guarantee of Jesus (Yeshua) that, if we are His, we will be able to endure to the end and His rewards will make it all worthwhile.[1]

2. YESHUA OVERCAME THE WORLD (JOHN 16:33)

"I have told you these things, so that in me you may have peace. In this world you will have trouble. But take heart! I have overcome the world."

3. WE CAN OVERCOME THE WORLD BY OUR FAITH (1 JOHN 5:4)

"For whatsoever is born of God overcometh the world: and this is the victory that overcometh the world, even our faith."

4. REWARDS FOR THE OVERCOMERS

There are nine (9) rewards promised to every believer that overcomes the world. A reward is a thing given in recognition of one's service, effort, or achievement. Let's take a look at the rewards that are promised to believers when the overcome the world or endure until the end:

---

[1] http://www.gotquestions.org/Bible-overcomer.html

REWARD #1
EATING FROM THE TREE OF LIFE

Revelation 2:7

"To him who overcomes I will give to eat from the tree of life, which is in the midst of the Paradise of God."

Eating from the Tree of Life is a reminder of the _____ for Adam (and all mankind) when the Lord placed him in the Garden of Eden. The tree of life was in the midst of the Garden and it was there for man in his _____ state before the fall.

Adam was restricted access to this tree because he fell from his glorious state – which was the image of God – by eating from the tree opposing the Tree of Life which was the Tree of the Knowledge of Good and Evil. Perhaps the fruit from every tree in the Garden of Eden was good for man to eat for his natural sustenance, but the fruit from the two specifically named trees were there to impact his spiritual condition. The Tree of Life was to _____ the image of God and the Tree of the Knowledge of Good and Evil was there to _____ that image.

The overcomer will have _____ _____ to the Tree of Life sustaining the image of God for all faithful believers. He will not be affected by the Second death, which is eternal separation from the life of God. The Tree of Life is indicative of _____ and divine blessing.

"_____ are they that do His commandments, that they may have right to the Tree of Life, and may enter in through the gates of the city. For without are dogs, and sorcerers, and whoremongers, and murderers, and idolaters, and whosoever loveth and maketh a lie" (Revelation 22:14-15).

REWARD #2
THE CROWN OF LIFE

Revelation 2:10-11

"I will give you the *crown of life*. He who has an ear, let him hear what the Spirit says to the churches. He who overcomes *shall not be hurt by the second death*" (Revelation 2:10-11).

This is what apostle James had to say about the crown of life: "Blessed is the man who endures temptation; for when he has been approved *(found consistent)*, he will receive the crown of life, which the Lord has promised to those who love Him" (James 1:12).

There are two Greek words describing two different types of crowns in the New Testament. One is the crown of a ruler—Greek *diadem*. The other is the crown of a _____—Greek *stephanos*: one who wins a race in the Greek athletic games. The Greek word "stephanos" is used here in Revelation 2:10 and James 1:12. The crown of life is a special reward given specifically for enduring persecution. The crown of life is for those who have the heart of a _____.

REWARD #3
EAT OF THE HIDDEN MANNA

Revelation 2:17

"He who has an ear, let him hear what the Spirit says to the churches. To him who overcomes I will give some of the *hidden manna* to eat."

Hidden manna speaks of having an increased capacity to be fed by revelation of the Word in this age and in the age-to-come. This manna will be given to us in fullness at the Marriage Supper.

God _____ His people in the wilderness with manna or "angel's food" (Ps.78:19-25). How much more will he sustain his people in his kingdom! We will be supernaturally sustained by God and eat heavenly sustenance even while living on the new earth. We will be able to eat interchangeably food on earth and food made in heaven. We will eat from the tree of life and manna from heaven while living on earth.

REWARD #4
A WHITE STONE WITH A NEW NAME WRITTEN ON IT

Revelation 2:17
"To him who overcomes… I will give him *a white stone*, and on the stone *a new name* written which no one knows except him who receives it"

Precious stones were given as awards to honor those who offered _____ _____ or in battle. Those receiving these stones were also given special privileges like receiving a gold medal. A white stone with one's name on it gave them admission to special events, including the games and feasts hosted by the government of the Roman Empire.

The stone (Gk *pshfos*) referred to a precious stone (diamond). White (Gk *leukos*) refers to "shining or glistening" (Matthew 17:2; Revelation 3:4-5; 6:11; 7:9, 13; 19:14). This stone may apply to various degrees of honor and privileges in the Marriage Supper of the Lamb. We will all have a different status at Yeshua's great banquet. The overcomer receives a new name to indicate his place in the kingdom rule and to describe their relationship with Yeshua.

REWARD #5
AUTHORITY OVER THE NATIONS

Revelation 2:26
"He who overcomes…to him I will give power over the nations"

This reward signifies that the overcomer will have _____ with Christ in the millennial kingdom (Revelation 19:15; 20:4).

2 Timothy 2:11, 12
It is a faithful saying: For if we be dead with him, we shall also live with him: If we suffer, we shall also *reign* with him: if we deny him, he also will deny us.

REWARD #6
CLOTHED IN WHITE GARMENTS

Revelation 3:5
"He who overcomes shall be clothed in white garments…"

The white garments express how God valued the dedication of the believer for living a righteous and holy life in this world. The "white" garment denotes brightness, thus being clothed in it gives the genuine believer the reward of a glowing recognition of honor in the kingdom of God. Yeshua rewards righteous living!

Revelation 19:8
"And to her it was granted to be arrayed in fine linen, clean and bright, for the fine linen is the _____ of the saints."

Matthew 13:43
"Then the righteous will shine forth as the sun in the kingdom of their Father."

A great multitude of believers received white garments for _____. You are not alone. Countless of other believers throughout history have chosen to live upright before a holy God!

Revelation 7:9, 14
"A great multitude…of all nations…and tongues, standing before the Throne…clothed with white robes …These are the ones who come out of the Great Tribulation, and washed their robes and *made them white in the blood of the Lamb.*"

REWARD #7
NAME WRITTEN IN THE BOOK OF LIFE

Revelation 3:5
"I will not blot out his name from the Book of Life; but I will confess his name before My Father and before His angels."

The Son of God, Yeshua haMashiach (Jesus the Christ), gives eternal security to those who genuinely believe and made their calling and election sure by adding to their faith (2 Peter 1:10-11). He will thus confess our names to the Father and before the congregation of holy angels. The overcomer's name will be reverberating through the ears of holy angels and his name shall be eternally archived in the annals of heaven's history book of life never to be blotted out. The believer will pass the investigative trial in the courtroom of heaven and have eternal entrance into the kingdom of God.

REWARD #8
A PILLAR IN GOD'S TEMPLE

Revelation 3:12

"He who overcomes, I will make him a pillar in the temple of My God, and he shall go out no more. And I will write on him the name of My God and the name of the City of My God, the New Jerusalem, which comes down out of heaven from My God. And I will write on him My new name."

All believers are part of God's spiritual temple (Eph. 2:21, 22), but some will be pillars who hold a position of _____, _____ and _____ in the Millennium.

Pillars are functional in helping to bear the weight of a building. They are ornamental in enhancing its beauty. They are social in declaring the honor of those who did heroic deeds of _____, _____ and _____. They are permanent thus speak of stability. They represent the "standard bearers" of the New Jerusalem as the seraphim are guardians of God's Throne.

The genuine believer who overcomes the world will be given a place of service and honor before God. The threefold reference to *the name* gives a guarantee of eternal security in Christ.

1. The name of My God shows _____.
2. The name of the city of My God, the New Jerusalem, shows heavenly _____.
3. His new name indicates _____ with Christ.

REWARD #9
SHARING CHRIST'S THRONE

Revelation 3:21

"To him who overcomes I will grant to sit with Me on My throne, even as I also overcame, and am set down with my Father on His throne."

The church of Laodicea had to overcome _____. The lukewarm believer is _____, _____ and does not realize his need. When a believer can overcome his battle against spiritual lethargy and _____ *faith*, Yeshua promised to reward him by sitting with Him on His throne. This refers to reigning with Christ in His kingdom. In order to receive this reward you must become passionate about your faith, catch on fire for God and maintain a high level of enthusiasm for living for the King. Christ does not want anyone ruling with Him that may get _____ with implementing kingdom principles.

CONCLUSION: These promised rewards should keep us motivated, encouraged and focused on our faith in Jesus Christ. There's a great day coming when all eyes shall see Him and when we all shall appear before the judgment seat of Christ. Are you looking forward to the Marriage Supper of the Lamb? Are you anticipating receiving these great rewards from the King of kings?

Although the world unleashes a constant, aggressive attack against the believers, we can rest assure that "greater is He that is in us than he that is in the world" (1 John 4:4). God has well equipped us for the fight. We are well armed for battle. Let us walk in the faith and assurance that the enemy is already defeated!

Spiritual warfare is not just for the promises of God for this life but for all the many blessings that God has awaiting us in the life to come – Life Eternal. Let's fight a good fight and lay hold unto eternal life (1 Timothy 6:12). We have so much to look forward to and it's worth the fight!

LIVE
Live In Victory Everyday

SPIRITUAL WARFARE
7 HIGH PLACES OF CULTURAL INFLUENCE

"When the righteous are in authority the people rejoice; but when a wicked man rules, the people groan" (Proverbs 29:2).

RELIGION
Where people worship God in spirit and in truth or settle for a religious ritual

FAMILY
Where either the blessing or curse is passed onto successive generations

EDUCATION
Where truth or lies about God and His creation are taught

MEDIA
Where information is interpreted through the lens of good and evil

ARTS & ENTERTAINMENT
Where values and virtues are celebrated or distorted

GOVERNMENT
Where evil is either restrained or endorsed

BUSINESS
Fuels and funds all the other mountains. Where people build for the glory of God or the glory of man. Where resources are consecrated for the kingdom of God or captured for the powers of darkness. Those who lead this mountain controls what influences our culture.

designed by Agape Advertisemnet Inc.

Spiritual Warfare—Defeat Your Enemy and Live a Victorious Life

Chart produced by Bishop Antonio M. Palmer 9.18.2013

Satan [Lucifer], who led an unsuccessful revolt in heaven with a third of the angels in heaven (Rev 12:2, 9) fell like lightning from heaven (Luke 10:18) and became the god of this world (2 Cor 4:4) and the prince of the power of the air (Eph 2:2) after causing Man to disobey God's command. Now he is the chief antagonist of the kingdom of God and of His Christ and has set up an army of fallen angels and demons to oppose the Lord and His work.

Principalities

Fallen angels who have oversight of nations. They would correspond with the rank of generals. I call them "Federal Devils." They cause "national" upheavals. They influence kings, princes, presidents, prime ministers, national/federal legislators and ambassadors.

Powers

These are the "privates" who are demons wanting to possess human beings. They also manipulate individuals and families to stay bound to certain generational curses. They are the "strongmen" who set up strongholds in individuals, families and communities and persuade them to tolerate certain social immoralities and injustices.

Rulers *of the darkness of this world*

These are fallen angels who have charge of Satan's "world" influences or systems of this world." They control media, arts and entertainment, education, governments, businesses/economy, and religions.

Spiritual Wickedness *in high places*

Also known as "spiritual forces of evil in heavenly places." They fight over words in the atmosphere and try to bring hindrances to prayers, prophecies and the promises of God. They attempt to hold back the gospel of the Kingdom of God from people and nations.

"For we wrestle not against flesh and blood, but against principalities, against powers, against rulers of the darkness of this world, against spiritual wickedness in high places" (Ephesians 6:12).

www.KingdomCelebrationCenter.com

Spiritual Warfare—Defeat Your Enemy and Live a Victorious Life

DEMONIC SPIRITS THAT BIND INDIVIDUALS AND FAMILIES

Spirit of Murder	Religious Spirit	Spirit of Lust	Spirit of Pride	Mental Health	Spirit of Unforgiveness	Occultic Spirits	Spirit of Infirmity	Spirit of Vices
Murder	Islam	Lust	Pride	Fear	Unforgiveness	Witchcraft	Any Kind of disease or illness	Alcoholism
Hate	Jehovah's Witness	Fornication	Arrogance	Depression	Bitterness	Fortune Telling	Death	Cocaine
Rage	Mormonism	Adultery	Haughtiness	Torment	Jealousy	Tarot Cards	Anorexia	Heroin
Anger	Hinduism	Pornography	Rebellion	Dread	Resentment	Ouija Boards	Bulimia	Meth
Violence	Buddhism	Pedophilia	Blasphemy	Hopelessness	Stubbornness	Automatic Writing	Insomnia	Marijuana
Death	Confucianism	Rape	Control	Despair	Envy	Seances	Epilepsy	LSD
Revenge	Shintoism	Incest	Possessiveness	Insecurity	Hard-heartedness	Mediums	Gluttony	Anti-prescription drugs
Destruction	Sikhism	Homosexuality	Contention	Paranoia	Anger	Necromancy	Abnormal amounts of lethargy or sleepiness	
Darkness	Jainism	Transvestism	Quarreling	Suspicion		Astrology		
Suicide	Zoroastrianism	Transexuality	Judgmental	Distrust		Hypnotism		
Abortion	Spiritualism	Sexual Orgies	Selfish	Loneliness		I Ching		
Jealousy	Hare Krishna	Wife Swapping	Narcissistic	Shyness		Crystals		
Sadism	Christian Science	Prostitution	Unbelief	Discouragement		Satanism		
Fighting	Scientology	Bestiality	Skepticism	Passivity		Voodoo		
	Kabbalah	Sadomasochism	Greed	Lying		Channelling		
	Unification Church		Poverty	Deceit		Astral Projection		
	Freemasonry		Paranoia	Antisocial		Transcendental Meditation		
	The Children of God		Deceit	Compulsive		ESP		
	EST		Mockery	neurotic behavior		New Age		
	Eckanar			Phobias				
	The Forum			Madness				
	The Way Int'l			Insanity				
	Theosophy			Schizophrenia				
	Rosicrucianism			Multiple Personalities				
	Atheism			Hearing Voices				
	Legalism			Mind Control				

Source: www.Bible-Knowledge.com/different-kinds-of-demonic-spirits.com

Rev10/2023 — 95

Names, Titles, Descriptions and Symbols of Satan in the Bible

By Agapegeek

http://agapegeek.wordpress.com/2010/08/16/names-titles-descriptions-and-symbols-of-satan-in-the-bible/

This is a list of the Names, Titles, Descriptions, Types and Symbols for our enemy Satan in the Bible that I have found. This is a living document of references to Satan. It will change and be updated as I find additional scriptures. A **Name** is a direct reference to Satan. A **Title** is a given direct identifying appellation signifying status or function. A **Description** is something that represents something in words. A **Type** is a real named person, place or thing that can be viewed to apply to a spiritual individual not named. A **Symbol** is a natural object that describes characteristics or features of a spiritual being you cannot see.

Name, Title, Symbol, Type for Satan	Description	Scripture Reference
666	The Number of the Beast	Revelation 13:18
Abaddon	Destroying Angel	Revelation 9:11
Accuser of the Brethren	Legal Opponent in Court of Law	Revelation 12:10
Adversary	The Opponent to the Church in a Lawsuit	1 Peter 5:8
Angel of Light	Impersonator, Actor, Stage Performer; Masquerader	2 Corinthians 11:14
Angel of the Bottomless Pit	Ruler of the Darkness	Revelation 9:11
Anointed cherub that coverth	The Winged Angelic Defender	Ezekiel 28:14
Antichrist	Opponent of the Messiah	1 John 4:3
Apollyon	Greek Name of Hebrew Abaddon; Destroyer	Revelation 9:11
Balaam	False Teacher	Jude 1:11
Bear	Kingdom of Satan Symbol	Revelation 13:2
Beast	Dangerous Animal; Venomous	Revelation 14:9-10; Revelation 16:10
Beelzebub	Lord of the Flies; A god of Babylon	Matthew 12:24, 27; Mark 3:22; Luke 11:15, 18-19
Belial	Worthless One	2 Corinthians 6:15
Bird, Hateful	Loveless	Revelation 18:2
Bird, Unclean	Foul,	Revelation 18:2
Blasphemer	Name of the One Who Vilifies God	Revelation 13:1
Cain	Murderer from the Beginning	Jude 1:11

Name	Meaning	Reference
Chief of Demons	Prince of demonic gods	Luke 11:15
Deceiver	The One Who Deceives	Revelation 12:9
Devil	False Accuser; Slanderer	Matthew 4:1-11; Matthew 25:41; Luke 4:2-13; Luke 9:42; John 8:44; Acts 10:38; Ephesians 4:27; James 4:7; 1 John 3:8; Revelation 2:10
Dragon	Fabulous Serpent	Revelation 12:7
Dragon, Great	Powerful Fabulous Serpent	Revelation 12:9
Enemy	Adversary	Matthew 13:39
Esau	Lord Hates	Malachi 1:2-3; Romans 9:13
Evil One	Malicious; Wicked One	John 17:15
False Light	The Opposite TRUTH of True Light Jesus	1 John 2:8
Father	Male Parent	John 8:44; Acts 13:10
Father of Lies	Fabricator of truth	John 8:44
Frog	Unclean Spirit	Revelation 16:13
Fox	Cunning Spirit	Luke 13:32
Goat, He (devils)	Devils (Hebrew Word for He Goat)	Leviticus 17:7; 2 Chronicles 11:15
God of this World	Ruler of the Night	2 Corinthians 4:4
Great Red Dragon	Serpent of Increased Power	Revelation 12:3
Herod	A Type of Satan the Murdering King	Luke 13:31
Judas	Judah The Betrayer of Messiah	John 6:70-71; John 13:2
King of Babylon	Ruler of Jerusalem	Isaiah 14:4
King of the Bottomless Pit	Ruler of the Darkness	Revelation 9:11
King of Tyrus	Ruler of the Rock	Ezekiel 28:12
Leopard	Kingdom of Satan Symbol	Revelation 13:2
Lesser Light	Moon who Rules the Night of Darkness	Genesis 1:16
Leviathan	Serpent Monster of Babylon	Isaiah 27:1
Liar	Falsifier; Deceiver	John 8:44
Lion	Kingdom of Satan Symbol	Revelation 13:2
Little Horn	Rising King	Daniel 8:9-11
Lucifer	Bright and Morning Star	Isaiah 14:12-14
Man of Sin	Man faced Trespasser	2 Thessalonians 2:3-4
Moon	Ruler of the Night	Psalm 136:9; Rev 12:1
Murderer	Man Killer	John 8:44
Oppressor	He Who Makes Sick	Acts 10:38
Power of Darkness	Superhuman Ruler of the Night	Colossians 1:13-14

Prince of the Devils	Ruler of Evil Spirits	Matthew 9:34; Matthew 12:24; Mark 3:22
Prince of the Kingdom of Persia	Ruler of the nation of Babylon	Daniel 10:13
Prince of the Power of the Air	Ruler of the Authority of Spoken Words	Ephesians 2:1-2
Prince of this World	Ruler of the Evil Darkness	John 12:31-32; John 14:30; John 16:11; 1 Corinthians 2:6-8;
Roaring Lion	Powerful Sounding King of the Beasts	1 Peter 5:8
Ruler of the Darkness	Moon who Rules the Night	Ephesians 6:12
Satan	The Accuser	Mark 1:13; Revelation 12:9
Seducing Spirit	Imposter; Deceiver	1 Timothy 4:1
Serpent	Symbolic Name for Satan	Genesis 3:1; Revelation 12:15
Serpent, Old	Symbolic Name for Satan; First Ruler of the earth	Revelation 12:9; Revelation 20:2
Son of Perdition	Destruction's Child	2 Thessalonians 2:3
Son of the Morning	Satan a son of God's Early Light	Isaiah 14:12-14
Spirit, Foul	Perverted Spiritual Being	Revelation 18:2
Spirit, the	Satan a spiritual being	Ephesians 2:2
Spirit, Unclean	Leprous Spiritual Being	Luke 9:42; Revelation 16:13
Star	Angel Cast Down to Earth	Revelation 9:1
Star, Wandering	He Who Departs the Path	Jude 1:13
Tempter	He Who Proves and Tests	Matthew 4:3
Thief	Robber; Burglar	Matthew 24:43; Luke 12:39; John 10:10
Wicked	Law Breaker; Evil Degenerate	2 Thessalonians 2:8; Ephesians 6:16

www.ingramcontent.com/pod-product-compliance
Lightning Source LLC
Chambersburg PA
CBHW081754100526
44592CB00015B/2424